For more than 25 years, The Institute of Internal Auditors has looked to The Research Foundation to define leading internal audit practices and to promote the profession to academic institutions. The Foundation's board of trustees recently redefined their mission as:

"To be the recognized leader in sponsoring and disseminating research, to assist and guide internal auditing professionals and others, in the areas of risk management, controls, governance processes and audit practices."

The Research Foundation is committed to:

- Defining internal auditing practices as performed by global leaders in research reports.
- Educating practitioners, educators, and the general public about the merits of internal auditing.
- Distributing materials on the benefits of internal auditing to organizational leaders and clients.

To continue to benefit from this ongoing effort and to help The Foundation fund top-quality research studies and educational programs for internal auditors worldwide, join the Master Key Program. For $1,000, your organization can become a subscriber and receive all Research Foundation publications and research reports as soon as they come off the press.

Master Key subscribers will receive titles like:

- *Electronic Systems Assurance and Control*
- *Adding Value: Seven Roads to Success*
- *A Balanced Scorecard Framework for Internal Auditing Departments*
- *Enterprise Risk Management: Pulling It All Together*
- *Mergers, Acquisitions, and Divestitures: Control and Audit Best Practices*

To subscribe to the Master Key Program, call +1-407-937-1356 or e-mail: research@theiia.org

---

Count on The IIA Research Foundation to help you perfect your profession and empower your success. Subscribe today.

To order individual copies of Research Foundation reports:
Online: www.theiia.org under The IIA
E-mail: iiapubs@pbd.org

MERGERS, ACQUISITIONS, AND DIVESTITURES: CONTROL AND AUDIT BEST PRACTICES

By Georges M. Selim, Ph.D., FIIA (UK),
Sudi Sudarsanam, Ph.D., ACIB,
and Michael K. Lavine, CIA, CISA, CGFM

The Institute of Internal Auditors Research Foundation

Disclosure

The IIA publishes this document for informational and educational purposes. This document is intended to provide information, but is not a substitute for legal or accounting advice. The IIA does not provide such advice and makes no warranty as to any legal or accounting results through its publication of this document. When legal or accounting issues arise, professional assistance should be sought and retained.

The Professional Practices Framework for Internal Auditing (PPF) was designed by The IIA Board of Directors' Guidance Task Force to appropriately organize the full range of existing and developing practice guidance for the profession. Based on the definition of internal auditing, the PPF comprises *Ethics* and *Standards, Practice Advisories,* and *Development and Practice Aids,* and paves the way to world-class internal auditing.

This guidance fits into the Framework under the heading *Development and Practice Aids*.

ISBN 0-89413-497-3
02338 10/02
First Printing

CONTENTS

List of Tables

List of Figures

ABOUT THE AUTHORS

Georges M. Selim, Bcom, Mcom, Ph.D., FIIA (UK), is Professor of Internal Auditing and Director of the Centre for Internal Auditing at Sir John Cass Business School (formerly the City University Business School) - London, UK. He is a former member of the Executive Committee and Board of Directors of The IIA (1993-1996), and a former President of The IIA-UK (1991-92).

In 1991, he was appointed Deputy Dean of the Business School (1991-93) and previous to that was appointed Sub-Dean (1988-91). In his capacity as Deputy Dean he led the development of the Management MBA in Europe and the Middle East.

Professor Selim has written numerous books and articles and has lectured extensively on internal auditing, accounting, and corporate governance in Europe, the Far East, and U.S. He is the independent chairman of the audit committees of a large UK government agency and of a large UK government department.

Professor Selim was elected the "1992 Educator of the Year" by The IIA and was awarded in 2000 — with David McNamee — the John B. Thurston Award for Literary Excellence for their paper titled "The Next Step in Risk Management."

Professor Selim can be reached by e-mail at G.M.Selim@city.ac.uk.

Sudi Sudarsanam, BSc, MSc (Physics), MSc (Finance), Ph.D. (Accounting & Finance), ACIB (Associate of the Institute of Bankers, London), is Professor of Finance & Corporate Control at the Cranfield University School of Management in the UK. He is also Director of the Finance Track on the MBA programme at Cranfield. He was previously Professor of Finance & Accounting at the City University Business School, London.

Professor Sudarsanam is the author of *The Essence of Mergers and Acquisitions* (Prentice Hall, 1995), a leading textbook on this subject. His second book, *Creating Value through M & A: The Challenges*, is due for publication in 2003, to be published by Prentice Hall.

Professor Sudarsanam has published over 20 articles in top refereed journals in the U.S. and Europe on M & A, corporate restructuring, financial analysis, and corporate governance and in professional journals, and presented over 40 international conference papers. He is an Associate Editor of the *Journal of Business Finance & Accounting*.

Professor Sudarsanam can be reached by e-mail at P.S.Sudarsanam@Cranfield.ac.uk.

Michael K. Lavine, MSc., M.S., B.S., CIA, CISA, CGFM, is a Visiting Assistant Professor of Computer and Information Sciences and Accounting at Towson University in Baltimore, Maryland. He is also Managing Director of Business Solutions International, LLC (www.bizsolutionsintl.com) and provides a variety of consulting and training services to clients in the U.S., Europe, and Africa.

Professor Lavine has 12 years of diverse experience as an internal, IT, and external auditor — most recently with PricewaterhouseCoopers, LLP. Currently, he is completing his Ph.D. studies in IT Security at Sir John Cass Business School, City University in London, England.

Professor Lavine has published a number of articles in IT auditing, accounting information systems, and fraud in such journals as *The CPA Journal*, *The Review of Business Information Systems* and *The Review of Accounting Information Systems*.

Professor Lavine can be reached by e-mail at mlavine@aol.com.

ACNOWLEDGMENTS

The researchers would like to express their deep appreciation for the support they received from The Institute of Internal Auditors Research Foundation (IIARF), especially Susan Lione, Senior Research Manager, and Gareth Evans, Project Management Team Leader. We also value the feedback and comments received from John Copley, Gareth Evans, Betty Ann Blandon, Kasey K. Kiplinger, Claire Beth Nilsen, and Mark L. Salamasick. Professors Istemi Demirag and John Forker at Queens University, Belfast, Northern Ireland, UK, provided comments and suggestions which were gratefully received.

In addition, the researchers would like to give special thanks to the chief audit executives, senior internal auditors, and senior managers in the following organizations for their help, support, and assistance with this project:

Akzo Nobel, Holland
Argo Wiggins Appleton, UK
Astra Zeneca, UK
Bank of America, USA
Bank One, USA
British American Tobacco, UK
Boeing, USA
Bon Secours Health System, USA
Carlson Wagonslit, France
Daimler-Chrysler, Germany
Entergy, U.S.
Exxon Mobil, U.S.
KPMG, UK
Lattice Group, UK
Lloyds TSB, UK
Lucent Technologies, U.S.
Microsoft, U.S.
Olivetti, Italy
Rouse Corporation, U.S.
Starwood, U.S.
UniCredito Italiano, Italy
Westinghouse, U.S.

Furthermore, the researchers would also like to acknowledge as well as express their sincere gratitude to the chief audit executives in the following organizations for their time and effort in helping the researchers interview senior executives in other parts of their organizations:

Bank of America, U.S.
Boeing, U.S.
Bon Secours Health System, U.S.
Entergy, U.S.
Lucent Technologies, U.S.
Microsoft, U.S.
Rouse Corporation, U.S.
Starwood, U.S.

Special acknowledgment must be made of Dr. Robert Melville, one of the original researchers, for his contribution to the literature review carried out as part of this research project. For work reasons, Dr. Melville had to withdraw from the project team.

Finally, special thanks to Chris Radford, Dennis Gound, and Hilary Browne for their secretarial support.

Project Management Team

The Institute of Internal Auditors
Research Foundation Staff

CHAPTER 1 INTRODUCTION AND EXECUTIVE SUMMARY

Introduction

Empirical evidence assembled by several studies in the United States, United Kingdom, and other countries points to a high rate of failure of mergers and acquisitions to create value for the shareholders of acquiring firms. The failure can occur at any of the five main stages that characterize the merger and acquisition process: strategic planning, specific acquisition/divestiture planning, deal structuring and negotiation, post-acquisition integration, and post-acquisition/divestiture audit. Failure can stem from flawed acquisition strategy, poor takeover bid strategies and tactics driven by the deal making momentum, and post-acquisition poor implementation. There are similar and parallel stages in divestitures with corresponding risks of failure.

Success of mergers, acquisitions, and divestitures (M, A, & D) as a means of achieving the strategic objectives of firms requires a deep understanding of the sources of value creation, the dynamics of takeover or divestitures, and the organizational and human aspects of post-acquisition or post-disposal situations. The risk of failure at each of the five stages mentioned above needs careful evaluation and calibration.

Traditionally, internal audit has been involved in due diligence, with its role being limited, in the majority of cases, to accounting issues.

In addition, internal audit in leading edge organizations has taken part in deal structuring and negotiation, post-acquisition integrating, and last but not least post-acquisition audit. The limits and boundaries of internal audit's role in all of the above need exploring in order to identify the added value services provided and the means for delivering such services.

Need for the Study

The need for the project arises from the increasing importance of M, A, & D to corporate strategy, the record of failure of such strategies in creating value and the apparent lack of understanding of the interdependence of the various stages in the process. This lack of understanding on the part of those charged with evolving and implementing M, A, & D strategies may have contributed to the widely reported failure of many acquisitions and where business units were divested at less than their real market value. It also suggests that proper risk assessment and control mechanisms were absent in many of these acquisitions/ divestitures.

This research will highlight the role of internal audit in assessing the risk attached to the different stages of the M, A, & D process. By providing a proper and objective evaluation of business risk, internal audit can challenge and constrain the more exuberant acquisition strategies driven by pure financial engineering, deal frenzy, and market fads. Thus it can contribute to an improved evaluation of acquisition opportunities consistent with the strategic needs of the firm and its strengths and weaknesses thereby minimizing the risk of overpayment to target shareholders, as well as the risk of poor integration of the acquired targets.

Divestitures present different but somewhat overlapping challenges. Divestiture may be the sale of an existing division of a company or of an acquired company immediately following an acquisition. While divestitures in general do not give rise to integration problems, they need to be evaluated from the firm's strategic perspective and carefully valued. Careful evaluation of the rationale for the divestiture, the mode of divestiture, negotiation with prospective buyers, and the price at which the divested part will be sold are all matters in which internal auditors can contribute useful input. There is a need to evaluate the current role played by internal auditors in the divestiture process and to explore ways of enhancing that role.

Research Methodology Employed

The study of internal auditors' role in mergers, acquisitions and divestitures (M, A, & D) was commissioned by The Institute of Internal Auditors Research Foundation (IIARF) in July 1999. The researchers carried out the fieldwork during the second half of 2000 and the first half of 2001. The fieldwork covered organizations in the United States and Europe. Internal auditors and senior managers from organizations spanning six countries contributed — through interviews — to this study. Models were derived from literature reviews and validated through interviews. Mid-2001, the researchers summarized the research results to date and — with the assistance of the IIARF technical staff — displayed this information through The IIA's Web site (http://gain2.org/mergers). Feedback from respondents was used to further develop the research findings. Full details of the methodology employed can be found in Appendix II.

Findings

The research findings, which are based on interviews carried out in 22 organizations, can be summarized as follows:

1. **Deal structuring and negotiations.** Internal auditors in 18 organizations are engaged in:

   - Carrying out due diligence assignments. Assignments that are carried out in some instances with other functions, such as finance, human resources (HR), information systems/information technology (IS/IT), etc.
   - Review and audit the risk assessment functions in the target company.
   - Provide independent validation of the assumptions used in pricing target.

   In addition, internal auditors in 15 organizations would also wish to offer additional services so as to:

   - Review and evaluate financial models used.
   - Ensure awareness of regulatory and other compliance matters.
   - Review and evaluate the process used to regulate the negotiation and deal-making stage.
   - Carry out a cultural audit of target firm.
   - Advise on the integration of financial, personnel, and organizational policies, and on developing these policies.

2. **Post-acquisition integration.** Internal auditors in 19 organizations are:

   - Participating in integration project management teams or task forces with other functions.
   - Auditing internal controls and risk management systems in the company to be acquired.
   - Assisting in developing and implementing plans to integrate internal audit (IA) of merging firms.
   - Agreeing timetables and benchmarks/key indictors for transition with operating units and audit progress against these.
   - Identifying communication gaps between acquiring and acquired businesses and different levels of staff during transition.
   - Evaluating business stability during integration.
   - Alerting HR to key personnel retention problems.

In addition, internal auditors in 16 organizations would also prefer to provide these additional services:

- Helping communication with acquired company staff regarding systems, procedures, risk management, etc.
- "Size up" the acquired company to see how it is run.
- Prepare a checklist of activities necessary to "actualize" expected value from the acquisition
- Play a consulting role to functions carrying out integration.
- Advise on the approaches to issues, such as HR, in planning the transition.

3. **Post-acquisition audit (as a special audit).** Internal auditors in only nine organizations are performing:

- Risk-based audit of policies, procedures, and controls in acquired company.
- Audit the post-acquisition appraisal system.
- Audit integration process to identify control weaknesses and to learn lessons using as a benchmark the final business case for the acquisition.
- Assess performance against benchmarks, e.g., balance scorecard and action plans.
- Work with M & A function to investigate whether the specific goals of the acquisition have been achieved, i.e., market share, profitability, etc.
- Prepare "Lessons Learned" document about integration process.
- Develop standards and checklists for the governance of stand-alone acquired subsidiaries.

Additional services that internal auditors in 17 organizations (77% of all organizations surveyed) felt they can offer their organizations are:

- Moving to continuous monitoring as done during merger transitions rather than the periodic normal audit.
- Auditing the organizational learning process for the lessons learned from past acquisitions and ensure that learning is shared among different functions.
- Where post-acquisition review is done by business units, IA can train unit managers in carrying out these reviews.

It is at the remaining two stages — strategic planning and specific acquisition planning — that internal auditors, in a much smaller number of organizations, have a more limited role to play. These roles can be summarized as follows:

4. **Strategic planning.** Internal auditors in only six organizations, a minority of the total organizations surveyed, are carrying out:

   - Audit the process used to develop business case.
   - Audit the process to see how risk is assessed and managed.
   - Audit the control process, to investigate whether control issues were addressed in the planning process and/or planning and execution processes.
   - Provide consulting services to develop guidelines for M & A.

   In addition, some internal auditors in five organizations believe that additional services can be offered to their organizations, which should:

   - Ensure that there is a coherent planning process governing the M & A activities of the company.
   - Advise on systems and processes that could reduce acquisition risk.

5. **Specific acquisition planning.** Internal auditors in three organizations provide a:

   - Review strategic implications and audit the business case for the acquisition.
   - Look at special projects, e.g., I.T, to assess risk and provide internal consultancy.
   - Review the target company's control system in order to help ascertain whether or not they are buying a good business.

   Additional services that internal auditors in six organizations, just above a quarter of all organizations surveyed, consider could be included:

   - Audit the business processes of the target company.
   - Look at the assumptions underpinning model used to justify acquisitions/divestitures.
   - Review composition of acquisition team to ensure that it contains people who have the right attitude to deal making, analytical skills, and the right attitude to risk.
   - Investigate whether there is too much pressure on the team to do deals.
   - Provide unique advice on cross-border deals, e.g., workers' councils in Germany.

Divestitures

In the case of divestitures, the scene is much simpler, internal auditors are not involved at the stages of:

(i) Strategic planning
(ii) Post-divestiture audit

Furthermore, any reasonable internal audit involvement is restricted to the "deal structuring and negotiating stage." At this stage, internal auditors in eight organizations:

- Carry out a closing audit.
- Ensure no hidden liabilities remain with vendor.
- Identify undervalued assets; determine net worth prior to divestiture to help in pricing the deal.
- Carry out due diligence.
- Help identify any intentional and unintentional errors before transaction is completed.
- Advise on warranties and guarantees given by vendor.
- Advise on structuring the deal.
- Help identify targets for divestiture.
- Help prepare prospectus for sale.
- Ensure stability while divestiture is in progress.

In addition, a number of internal auditors in an equal number of organizations (8) believe that the following additional services can be provided to their organizations:

- Evaluate the organizational impact of the divestiture.
- Assess tax and compliance implications of divestiture.

Recommendations for a More Effective Internal Audit Role in Mergers and Acquisitions

Internal audit could play a greater role at the different stages of mergers and acquisitions (M & A) through:

- **Strategic planning**

  1. Making sure that there is a well-defined and well-structured strategic planning process.
  2. Addressing the risk assessment process within the strategic planning process.
  3. Advising on systems and processes that can mitigate acquisition risk.

- **Specific acquisition planning**

  1. Examining the business processes of target companies.
  2. Reviewing the composition of the acquisition team for representation and diversity of talents.
  3. Maintaining a line of communication with the acquisition team and executive management throughout the process.

4. Assessing the financial and other pressures on the acquisition team to make the deal.
5. In special circumstances, providing advice such as regulatory compliance.
6. Making staff resources available for special projects and the organization's internal M & A SWAT team.

- **Deal structuring and negotiation**

1. Conducting internal control reviews during due diligence.
2. Ensuring due diligence covers all necessary functional areas.
3. Reviewing and evaluating financial models and projections used by management.
4. Recommending go/no-go parameters for individual deal.
5. Advising management on integration issues and specific suggestions.
6. Assessing the "cultural fit" of the target organization.

- **Post-acquisition integration**

1. Reviewing and monitoring high, medium, and tactical integration plans and results.
2. Providing consulting services to aid the business functions leading the integration efforts, including the loaning out of staff to assist with the integration.

- **Post-acquisition audit**

1. Increasing the number and frequency of related audits.
2. Providing training to business unit managers that conduct post-acquisition reviews.
3. Implementing continuous monitoring of key performance indicators.
4. Reviewing communication mechanisms for lessons learned and organizational knowledge management.

Recommendations for a More Effective Internal Audit Involvement in Divestiture Activities

The low level of actual and preferred IA involvement in divestiture activities indicates that this is an area where auditors do not appear to have much of a role to play. However, the researchers strongly believe that the following recommendations merit careful consideration by IA units seeking to become involved with divestitures.

1. Continually review low-performing business units and offer practical operational suggestions for improvement including divestiture.
2. Evaluate the business strategy case and the shareholder value justification for the divestiture decision.

3. Scrutinize the deal for the aftereffects on the residual businesses, e.g., loss of key relationships with the divested component, alternative sources of services or input previously provided by the divested business, and the relative costs of retention versus disposal.
4. Examine the risk exposure that arises from the need to provide warranties and indemnities.
5. Advise on the appropriateness of the valuation models used to support the divestiture decision, the minimum acceptable price, etc.
6. Advise on the appropriateness of the consideration form received.
7. Advise the operating units undergoing "de-integration" of the divested components.

Prerequisites

To enhance the effectiveness of internal audit as recommended above, the researchers strongly believe that a number of prerequisites are essential for internal audit to acquire and have if they are to play an expanded role in M, A, & D. These prerequisites are:

1. In-depth understanding of the organization's operating businesses and activities.
2. Knowledge of the firm's corporate strategies and business models.
3. Good understanding of the various sources of risks to which business units are exposed.
4. Ability to see the "big picture" from an overall business and corporate perspective.
5. Organizational culture that values IA's input as a monitor, adviser, and internal consultant.
6. Awareness of IA's capabilities and resources for a proactive role by top management and the board.
7. IA being perceived as a source of authentic experience and knowledge with an established record of setting up, monitoring, and auditing systems, processes, and procedures.
8. Organizational culture that values IA's input as a monitor, adviser, and internal consultant.
9. Recognition of the usefulness of IA's contribution to improved systems and processes associated with risk management.
10. Good facilitation, interpersonal, and communication skills.

Means of Achieving the Prerequisites

These can be summarized as follows:

Table 1.1
Means of Achieving the Prerequisites

Prerequisite	Means of Achieving the Prerequisite
1.	Rotation of staff among different functions including IA to facilitate cross-functional migration and learning about the state-of-the-art issues and models.
2.	Recruitment of staff into internal audit with experience of functions such as finance, IT, corporate strategy, and HR, as well as experience of relevant operating businesses.
3.	Organizational incentive policies that encourage secondment to IA of staff from other functions and which does not impede career progression in their parent functions.
4.	Training in professional and personal skills such as facilitating, communicating, negotiating, consulting, and interpersonal.
5.	Communicate ("evangelize") to other functions in a non-intrusive, non-threatening way about how IA's skills and tools would benefit them, identifying how IA capabilities and experience can be exploited by other functions in the organization.
6.	Change IA's self-perception from mere watchdogs, monitors, and "nit-pickers" to facilitators, problem-solvers, and consultants.
7.	Convince top management of the need to allow IA to build up key resources for a proactive role in the organization.

The Structure of the Report

The research report consists of:

Chapter 1, which acts as a brief introduction to the study and which also includes an executive summary where the research findings, recommendations, prerequisites for delivering these recommendations, and the means for achieving these prerequisites are presented.

Chapter 2, where an overview of the literature pertaining to M, A, & D is presented.

Chapters 3 and 4, which cover the research findings, recommendations based on gap analysis, and prerequisites needed if internal audit is to deliver the added value services that are potentially within their capabilities.

Chapter 5, where researchers compare the research objectives with what has been achieved.

The research report contains a number of appendices covering: a glossary of terms, copies of the "aide-memoire," and Web pages. In addition, the research methodology used in carrying out this research study is included.

CHAPTER 2
DEVELOPING A MODEL OF INTERNAL AUDIT'S ROLE IN MERGERS, ACQUISITIONS, AND DIVESTITURES
A REVIEW OF PRIOR STUDIES

Introduction

The literature on M, A, & D in the U.S. and in other countries like the UK provide extensive evidence that a majority of M & A transactions fail to generate value for the acquirer shareholders. The odds of positive and significant value creation for acquirer shareholders are even less than 50%, what one could get with the toss of a coin. Thus M & A transactions are high-risk corporate transactions. The risk of failure is all the more egregious when one considers the value of M & A transactions, especially during merger waves such as the one during 1993-2000. At the height of this boom, the value of M & A deals involving U.S. corporations was $1.75 trillions. This huge level of activity was matched by deals done outside the U.S. (*Mergers & Acquisitions Almanac,* February 2001).

The huge investments made by companies in M & A, combined with the high risk of failure, call for a serious examination of the sources of risk in M & A transactions. If these sources can be identified, appropriate preventive or remedial countermeasures can be taken. These countermeasures both to minimize potential risk in advance of a transaction and to mitigate the risks after the deal are likely to take the form of robust systems, processes, and procedures within acquiring firms. Internal audit can play an important role in advising management on the development, implementation, and monitoring of these systems, processes, and procedures. This is a role that internal auditors are actively performing in organizations where they are striving to increase the value-added services to their organizations (Drent, 2002).

In this chapter we first provide an historical overview of the results of mergers and acquisitions from the shareholder perspective. We then review the literature on various aspects of mergers and acquisitions. The focus of this review is to identify the sources of risk associated with the five stages of M & A transactions from the strategic evaluation stage to the post-completion audit stage. Our review leads to the risk profile of these different stages. We then describe the potential role of IA in helping management manage these risks. This normative model forms the basis of our subsequent interview-based research into the actual role of IA. For the purpose of the interview, we prepare an aide-memoire that includes an exhaustive set of questions derived from our normative model of the IA's role in the management of M & A related risk.

Divestitures are much less complex transactions than mergers and acquisitions. They nevertheless raise risk-related issues at different stages. Our normative model and aide-memoire are extended to cover divestitures.

Do Mergers and Acquisitions Add or Destroy Shareholder Value?

Table 2.1 summarizes the results of numerous studies from the U.S. and the UK assessing the performance of acquirers in terms of shareholder value enhancement. Wealth gains are measured by abnormal returns, i.e., returns in excess of an appropriate benchmark return. Because of uncertainty over the appropriate benchmark, researchers have used a variety of benchmarks. Table 2.1 provides clear evidence that shareholders of acquirers experience wealth losses on average, or at best, break even. On the other hand, shareholders of target companies are better off with abnormal returns in the order of 20% to over 43%.

The poor wealth experience of acquirers is common to both the U.S. and the UK. It is also fairly consistent across a range of models. In many of the studies there is a sharp deterioration in acquirer performance several years after deal completion. Overall, mergers and acquisitions more often destroy, rather than enhance, value for the acquirer shareholders.

However, one striking aspect of the post-acquisition performance is that there is some variation in acquirer and target shareholder wealth performance across merger types. In the U.S., tender offers generate more wealth for the shareholders than mergers. In the UK, hostile acquisitions generate larger wealth gains than friendly mergers.

Table 2.1
Post-acquisition Shareholder Returns (%) in U.S. and UK Takeovers: Summary of Empirical Studies[1]
Panel A: U.S. Studies

Study (year)	Type of offer	Returns to target shareholders during takeover bid (%)[2]	Returns to bidder shareholders during takeover bid (%)	Returns to acquirer shareholders in (years) after acquisition (%)
Jensen & Ruback (1983)	Merger Tender	20 30	0 4	
Magenheim & Mueller (1988)	Merger Tender		-0.4 1.4	-28 (3) 9
Jarrell & Poulsen (1989)	Tender	29	1.0	
Franks, Harris, & Titman (1991)	Full sample Contested Uncontested	28 39 25	-1.0 -1.4 -0.9	0.1 (3) 0.0 0.3
Loderer and Martin (1992)	Merger Tender			0.0 (5) 0.0
Agrawal, Jaffe, & Mandelker (1992)	Merger			-10.3 (5)
Loughran & Vijh (1997)	Merger Tender			-16.0 (5) 43.0
Rao & Vermaelen (1998)	Merger Tender			-4.0 (3) 8.6

[1]The studies cited in the above table are reviewed in Appendix IV.

[2]Returns are actual returns less the returns to a benchmark portfolio, e.g., the market, similar sized firms, firms with similar market to book value of equity ratios or combinations of these in the form of multiple indices. The bid period includes a few days before announcement to a few days after and in some studies extends to the date of completion.

Table 2.1 (Cont.)
Panel B: UK Studies

Study (year)	Returns to target shareholders during takeover bid (%)	Returns to bidder shareholders during takeover bid (%)	Returns to acquirer shareholders in (years) after acquisition
Firth (1980)	28	-6.3	0.0 (3)
Franks & Harris (1989)	22	0.0	-12.6 (2)
Limmack (1991)	31	-0.2	-4.5 (2)
Sudarsanam et al. (1996)	29	-4.0	
Gregory (1997)[3]		-0.5	-8.2 (2)
Higson & Elliott (1998)[3]	38	0.4	-1.1 (2)

Our more detailed literature review in Appendix IV provides further evidence that deal structure makes a difference to value creation. Cash financed acquisitions create more value than stock for stock acquisitions. Thus choice of deal type or payment currency has a significant effect on wealth outcomes for shareholders. This points to the risk attached to inappropriate deal structures. Acquirers need to choose the deal structure very carefully.

The evidence presented above paints a rather unflattering picture of acquisitions and raises important questions about the reasons for acquisition failure. Failure can arise at any stage of the acquisition process, which may be divided for the purpose of this research, into five stages:

- Corporate strategy development
- Choice of acquisition as a strategic instrument and specific acquisition strategy
- Deal structuring and negotiation
- Post-acquisition integration
- Post-acquisition audit

[3]Gregory reports two-year returns of 1.7% for hostile and –10.4% for friendly acquirers. Higson & Elliott report 12.8% for hostile and –3.7% for friendly acquirers over two years after acquisition.

Our literature review covers studies dealing with these five stages and identifies the sources of risks to acquisition success. These sources inform our aide-memoire that forms the basis of our field research.

How Good is the Corporate Strategy Development Process?

Corporate strategy analysis has evolved in recent years through several paradigms — industry-structure driven strategy, competition among strategic groups, competence or resource-based competition, etc. (Thomas and Pollock, 1999). Under the industrial organization model of competition firms choose cost leadership or product differentiation within narrow segments or broad segments (the range of focus) but in general they respond to Porter's (1985) five forces — current rivalry, threat of entry of new competitors, threat of substitutes, the buyer power, and the seller power. Under this model firms make acquisitions to gain market power, economies of scale and scope, and internalize vertically linked operations to save on the cost of dealing with markets, thus adding further cost savings.

A firm's identification of its competitors may also depend on its cognitive perception of whether they are its competitors in some sense. Those firms operating in similar markets with similar current or potential capabilities may belong to the same strategic group and be regarded as competitors.

In recent years the resource-based view of competition has gained ground (Winter, 1995; Rouse and Daellenbach, 1999; Montgomery, 1994). The resource-based view is a conceptual framework for understanding firm level growth, using resources as the basic building blocks. These resources may be financial, human, intangible, physical, organizational, or technological. How a firm's management conceptualizes its resource base will define its strategy for growth.

Competitive advantage is now regarded as deriving from unique and idiosyncratic organizational resources and capabilities rather than from industry and market factors. Sustainable competitive advantage grows out of those valuable, rent-generating capabilities that cannot be easily imitated or substituted. Some members of an organization may be unaware which resources give it its unique competitive advantage. The resources and capabilities that give a firm its distinct competitive advantage are also known as its core competencies postulated by Prahalad and Hamel (1990) as the source of sustainable competitive advantage. These are embedded within organizational routines and cultures, i.e., "our way of doing things" and remain tacit.

Acquisitions may be interpreted within the resource-based model as a search for partners with complementary resources and capabilities, which can be leveraged with those of the acquirer to the enhanced competitive advantage of both firms. This model can also explain different types of acquisitions — related and unrelated or conglomerate.

The resource-based view of acquisitions raises important issues that may define the riskiness of those acquisitions. The acquiring firm may not be aware what its resources and capabilities are (Rouse and Daellenbach, 1999). It will be even less aware of the resources and capabilities of its intended merger partner. There will be further uncertainty about how complementary these capabilities are. Thus corporate strategy premised on exploitation of resources and acquisition strategy based on exploiting complementary resources may run the risk of being founded on incomplete knowledge. Traditional due diligence is unlikely to provide a reliable audit of the two firms' resources and capabilities and how they can leverage one another.

The tacit nature of resources and capabilities also means that it is difficult to quantify and value the benefits of the competitive advantage that they confer. Thus valuation may be seriously flawed. Post-acquisition integration of the complementary resources and capabilities is also a difficult exercise since the related knowledge is tacit and embedded within the organizations. This difficulty raises the risk of integration failure. "Acquirers can easily destroy value in the stand-alone business (of the acquired firm) by attempting to gain synergies that have little chance of occurring" (Sirower, 1998). "Moreover, the management of a buying firm should pay at least as much attention to issues of cultural fit during the pre-merger search process as they do to issues of strategic fit" (Chatterjee, Lubatkin, and Schweiger, 1992).

Our review also provides evidence that post-acquisition operating performance, stockholder value creation, and even the capacity for innovation are less likely in unrelated mergers than in related ones. Growth by unrelated acquisitions has resulted in the conglomerate firms being valued at a discount ('the conglomerate discount') to the sum of the values of the individual businesses (Servaes, 1996; Berger and Ofek, 1995). "Unrelated diversification is a bad idea from the point of view of the bidding firm's shareholders in the 1980s" (Morck, Shleifer, and Vishny, 1990). These authors argue that poor acquisitions are a manifestation of an agency problem in the acquirers, which is lacking in effective corporate governance. Thus poor acquisitions may be a consequence of, or aggravated by, governance failure.

How Good is the Company's Specific Acquisition Planning?

When companies plan for specific acquisitions, the proposed acquisition needs to be rigorously evaluated. The target selection process is concerned with not only the suitability of a firm as a target for an acquisition but also its availability at the right price and through the right deal structure. While a target may have the right "identikit" from a strategic and value creation perspective, there may be potential "showstoppers" that render pursuit of such a target either futile or too expensive.

Financial and nonfinancial characteristics of potential targets need to be carefully examined and a punctilious assessment of the risk of failure of an acquisition bid made. In making the assessment, the bidder must factor in the corporate governance structure, large block shareholding, relationship with customers and suppliers, etc., as relevant factors (Song and Walkling, 1993; and Shivdasani, 1993).

The target evaluation consists of both:

- Strategic evaluation, i.e., whether the intended target firm has the desired fit in terms of resources and capabilities with those of the bidder to ensure creation of sustainable competitive advantage and
- Value creation logic, i.e., whether the merger will generate returns over and above the cost of capital.

Value creation in mergers can be achieved through operational efficiencies and cost savings, revenue enhancement by more effective use of the merging firms' value chains or through leveraging their intangible assets like innovation, R & D, product development capabilities, etc. These sources of value differ in terms of the risk of non-realization. Cost savings are the easiest to estimate and realize and intangibles' leveraging to create new products and markets is the most difficult. Nevertheless, the real options on intangible assets may increasingly become the dominant source of competitive advantage.

In valuing potential targets, the options the investment provides need to be carefully considered (Smith and Triantis, 1994):

- Growth option to exploit the initial investment with a follow-on option, e.g., R & D followed by production,
- Flexibility option, e.g., opportunity to exploit assets like real estate in alternative future uses, and
- Divestiture option that mitigates the acquisition risk, e.g., acquisition followed by unbundling.

"In an increasingly uncertain world, real options have broad implications as a management tool. They will change the way you value opportunities. They will change the way you create value — both reactively and proactively" (Leslie and Michaels, 1997).

There may often be a tendency to hype up the potential scope for value creation. Availability and scope of cost savings, revenue enhancements, and real options are all based on forecasts that are often overoptimistic. The value creation logic must clearly spell out the assumptions underlying the forecasts as well as include alternative scenarios so that the risk profile of the proposed acquisition in terms of value creation can be realistically assessed. Both internal auditors and audit committees have a role in assessing such a risk profile (Deloitte and Touche, 1997).

What Are the Pitfalls in Deal Structuring and Negotiation?

This stage consists of:

- Choice of advisors to the deal such as investment bankers, lawyers, accountants, environmental consultants, etc.
- Obtaining and evaluating as much intelligence as possible about the target from the target as well as from other sources.
- Performing due diligence.
- Determining the range of negotiation parameters, including the "walkaway" price.
- Negotiating warranties and indemnities.
- Negotiating the positions of senior management of both firms in the post-merger dispensation.
- Developing the appropriate bid and defense strategies and tactics within the parameters set by the relevant regulatory regime, etc.

> The choice of advisors must be guided by the scope for conflicts of interest. Compensation contracts for advisors like investment banks need to be drawn up taking such conflicts into account, although custom and practice may influence the content of these contracts. Evidence shows that incentive contracts for investment banks may be perverse from the bidder's point of view (McLauglin, 1992). "The investment banks reaped higher fees as they negotiated higher acquisition prices regardless of the party (buyer or seller) they represented. This is especially troublesome for buying companies" (Kosnik and Shapiro, 1997).

Negotiations are conducted in an atmosphere where the bidder and the target may have private information that the other party does not have. Each can use this information advantage to gain favorable terms during negotiation. Effective techniques developed for negotiations under such circumstances must be followed to avoid buying a "lemon" (Dierickx and Koza, 1991). The negotiation team must be trained and experienced in these techniques. It must have the right balance among various relevant functions, top management, and line management. It must operate with clear guidelines and well-defined limits so that overpayment is avoided.

The due diligence process — which can be carried out by internal audit or external audit/ consulting firms — is unlikely to provide a comprehensive view of the target firm so the limits of due diligence must be kept in mind when assessing the information imbalance between buyer and seller. Traditionally, due diligence carried out by accountants and lawyers focused on accounting, tax, contractual liability issues, etc. However, in recent years the need to extend the scope of due diligence has become widely recognized. Due diligence is no longer just concerned with reducing risk. It should also contribute to effective management of the acquisition and the leveraging of the acquirer and acquired firms' resources and capabilities so that the goals of the acquisition can be realized.

Due diligence to be useful in valuing and negotiating deals and in effectively integrating and managing the acquired businesses needs to cover the following aspects of the target company:

- Commercial, e.g., competitive position, customer relations, patents
- Operational, e.g., production technology, processes and systems
- Financial and tax, e.g., historic accounting information, potential tax liabilities
- Legal, e.g., onerous contracts, product or environmental liabilities
- Human resource, e.g., compensation, training, employee relations
- Organizational, e.g., structure, management style, power distribution
- Information systems, e.g., performance, cost, complexity, compatibility

Due diligence teams must therefore draw upon a wide range of competencies both from within the acquirer and from external sources. Coordinating a team of such diverse specialists is itself a demanding and specialized function. IA can contribute to the setting up of the due diligence team and to its functioning by identifying the areas that need focusing and by keeping the team to a more rounded and holistic, rather than a functional, view of the acquisition. While mapping the areas that due diligence should focus on is relatively simple, gaining access to the required information is a formidable challenge.

In hostile deals and in deals with stock market listed companies, due diligence is likely to be deficient. Due diligence may also be inadequate in assessing the intangible assets of the target firm. Where the strategic logic is driven by such intangibles and value realization depends on the ability of the firms to leverage their intangible resources and capabilities, due diligence may be particularly weak. Absence of intelligence about the target should not induce complacency and encourage excessive optimism and overpayment in the hope of some mythical real options that may not exist. The sorry tale of the dotcom and telecom boom of the late 1990s provides a salutary reminder of the scope for such exuberant follies. Intangibles depend on people, teams, and organizational networks. Thus due diligence needs to include a human resource component (Overman, 1999).

We have noted that payment currency and type of acquisition — merger or tender offer or hostile or friendly — have significant consequences for shareholders. Unwarranted preoccupation with the accounting consequences of a deal may destroy value as happened with the AT&T's acquisition of NCR (Lys and Vincent, 1995). The tendency to be overgenerous with stock for stock offers, driven by current high stock valuation during a market boom, has to be checked and stock exchange ratios must be determined by realistic expectations of future growth as well as stock market conditions (Cooke, Gregory, and Pearson, 1994). The huge write-offs of goodwill by companies such as Vodafone, AOL-Time Warner, and Vivendi are very good examples of companies being overgenerous with their stock believing that because the acquisition was carried out through the use of shares, the company has not incurred any cost or value erosion. Risk of inappropriate payment currency or excessive acquisition premium must be mitigated by a careful justification based on realistic expectations. There needs to be a mechanism to provide this "reality check" (Eccles, Lanes, and Wilson, 1999).

Don't Start Counting the Chickens Yet — Risks in Post-acquisition Integration

At this very important stage, the objective is to put in place a merged organization that can deliver the strategic and value expectations that drove the merger in the first place. Integration has the characteristics of a change management program but here three types of change may be involved (Galpin and Robinson, 1997):

- Change of the target firm,
- Change of the acquiring firm, and
- Change in the attitude and behavior of both to accommodate coexistence or fusion of the two organizations

The integration process also has to be viewed as a project and the firm must have the necessary project management capabilities and program with well defined goals, teams, communication plans, deadlines, performance benchmarks, reward for meeting deadlines and benchmarks and sanctions for failure, etc. Such a methodical process can unearth problems and provide solutions so that integration achieves the strategic and value creation goals (Altier, 1997). A company must discover a pattern of change that builds momentum and promotes the shared vision, confidence, leadership capacity, and capabilities that will make the next change possible (Dickhout, 1997).

Merging firms' managers and employees may often be too distracted by the integration process to "keep an eye on the ball," i.e., they may neglect to "mind the store" and its customers who then will turn to the firms' competitors perhaps for good.

The integration time is also a time of great uncertainty for the managers and the workforce. They may be lured away by the competitors. Thus the integration program must assuage staff anxieties but also develop a key personnel retention policy. "Executives from an acquired firm are an intrinsic component of the acquired firm's resource base and their retention is an important determinant of post-acquisition performance. There are strong economic motives for initiating acquisitions but there are also strong social processes at work that may seriously affect the outcomes" (Canella Jr. and Hambrick, 1993).

One of the major problem areas in post-merger integration is the integration of the merging firms' information systems (IS). This factor needs to be considered at the specific acquisition stage itself (Buck-Lew, Wardle, & Pliskin, 1992). This is particularly important in mergers that seek to leverage each company's information on customers, markets, or processes with that of the other company as in a banking and insurance merger or in the merger of banks, e.g., the merger of the two largest Swiss banks — UBS and SBC. The compatibility of IS must be considered just as thoroughly as any strategic, operational, organizational, or political issue. "IS integration in M & A depends on a mix of both technical and organizational factors that force the new asset designers to consider the impact of the strategic objectives of the transaction on the integration cost in terms of financial, information, and human resources" (Giacomazzi, Panella, Pernici, and Sansoni, 1997). Organizational culture compatibility must also be considered alongside IS synergies (Weber and Pliskin, 1996). Hoffman (1997) discusses the turbulence faced by Boeing after its acquisition of McDonnell Douglas in carrying out IS integration.

Acquisitive firms must also consider post-merger integrative capabilities as a core competence. "GE Capital has been working to make acquisition a core capability" (Ashkenas, DeMonaco, and Francis, 1998). Development of such core competency requires setting up of robust systems and processes for integration. It also requires systems and processes that allow the lessons from past integration exercises to be archived, diffused, and internalized by the acquirer's organizational. Each integration experience should not be lost in organizational amnesia so that history needs to repeat itself.

The merger of Nations Bank and Boatmen in 1997 provides a good example of how internal auditors can help keep operations running smoothly during a merger and minimize the acquirer's financial loss due to customer defection or employee turnover (Trampe, 1998). Nations Bank's internal auditors were able to:

- Generate a number of cost savings opportunities by leveraging existing audit resources to avoid costly consulting fees, identifying potential problems and preventing unnecessary expenditures.
- Serve as goodwill ambassadors to Boatmen's employees easing their fears about the coming merger.
- Work closely with Nations Bank's stability team and document how normal operations would be maintained during the merger.
- Assist transition teams and line-of-business managers in implementing internal controls and the internal control aspects of major changes resulting from the merger.
- Ease the transition and save time.

How Did the Merger Go? The Post-merger Audit

This stage may often be neglected for several reasons, including:

- Lack of organizational emphasis on learning.
- Each deal considered so unique that past experience of mergers is deemed irrelevant.
- Lack of a centralized and ongoing function that is responsible for archiving the past and diffusion of learning.
- Past learning not codified but resides in individuals' experience with those individuals being co-opted into deal-making teams when necessary.
- Individuals' past experience is not systematically communicated but spread haphazardly through anecdotes and folklore within the organization.
- "The trail gone cold" — difficult to trace the acquired or merged firm since it is now part of a larger strategic business unit or subsidiary so lessons cannot be learned.

The importance of organizational learning to the success of future acquisitions needs much greater recognition, given the high failure rate of acquisitions (Light, 1999). Post-merger audit by internal auditors can be acquisition-specific as well as being part of an annual audit. IA has a major role in ensuring organizational learning and its dissemination.

Divestitures

The literature on divestitures is less extensive than that on M & A. It covers different types of corporate restructuring, including:

- Spin-off in which a firm decides to separate its fairly distinct businesses into separate companies with the shares in the new companies being allocated to the parent company shareholders.
- Equity carve-out in which a firm lists on a stock market minority shares in one of its subsidiaries so that subsidiary can be valued by the stock market on its own.
- Tracking stock in which a firm issues a separate parent company's class of shares to track the performance of one of its subsidiaries.
- Sell-off in which the firm sells a division or a subsidiary to another corporate buyer, a private equity firm, or managers in a management buyout (MBO).

The motivation for these restructuring activities is in general to reduce the conglomerate discount, improve focus, raise the transparency of the subsidiary's operations, improve managerial autonomy and incentive structures for the subsidiary managers, etc. (Afshar, Taffler, Sudarsanam, 1992; John and Ofek, 1995; Daley, Mehrotra, and Sivakumar, 1997). In general, these restructuring announcements are received positively by the stock market and post-restructuring performance of the spun-off or carved out subsidiary often improves

(Allen, 1998; Anslinger, Klepper, and Subramaniam, 1999). A spin-off may be used to unwind a poor acquisition. "Managers who undertake poor acquisition decisions can redeem themselves, at least partially, by subsequently divesting the unwise acquisition" (Allen, Lummer, McConnell, and Reed, 1995).

Divestitures present less complicated transactions than acquisitions since many of the risks we have identified above now pass on to the buyer. There is also no integration stage. Nevertheless, care must be taken in the following areas:

- Strategic evaluation and justification of the divestiture decision.
- Any potential loss of synergies, resources, and capabilities hitherto shared by the parent and the divested component and the impact on the parent's competitive advantage.
- Pricing — the right price must be negotiated.
- Issue of warranties and indemnities making sure these are appropriate to the risks being accepted by the selling firm.
- The consequences of de-integration — whether the selling firm will continue its supplier or buyer relationship and what risk this creates.
- Post-divestiture audit to ensure the strategic and financial goals of the divestiture decision have been realized.

Internal audit can play a significant role in the divestiture process. IA's past audit involvement with the businesses being considered for divestiture provides it with the information and a continuous perspective to contribute to evolving the criteria for the divestiture decisions as well as in evaluating the particular businesses for divestiture. IA can help evaluate the merits of the divestiture alternatives such as trade-sale, equity carve-out, spin-off, etc. It can also audit the systems and procedures for conducting the sale of a business through direct negotiation, auction, etc. and for the conduct of deal negotiations, e.g., the data rooms, adherence to confidentiality agreements, etc. As part of the auction process, companies carry out vendor audits and internal audit may become involved in the vendor due diligence.

Issue of warranties and indemnities needs to be carefully monitored to minimize post-divestiture exposure to extravagant claims of the buyer. While this is primarily a legal function, the content of warranties and indemnities requires careful vetting to ensure minimum exposure. Where divestitures form part of a program of strategic refocusing by the company, valuable lessons can be learned from previous divestitures to ensure that mistakes in valuation, negotiation, and risk management are avoided. This requires that IA should ensure that the lessons become part of the corporate memory and there are suitable training and other means of ensuring that this memory gets internalized and serves managers engaged in subsequent divestiture activity.

Epilogue

The above survey is more limited than the more extensive review of the literature reported in Appendix IV. Our literature review provided thc basis of the aide-memoire we prepared as a document for discussion with the interviewees in Stage 2 of the project. The aide-memoire can be found in Appendix III.

From this review the researchers were able to identify the sources of risks at the different stages of M, A, and D. These are graphically represented in Figures 2.1 to 2.6. Tables 2.2 to 2.8 provide more detailed illustrations of these risks.

Figure 2.1
Sources of Risks in Mergers and Acquisitions: General Overview

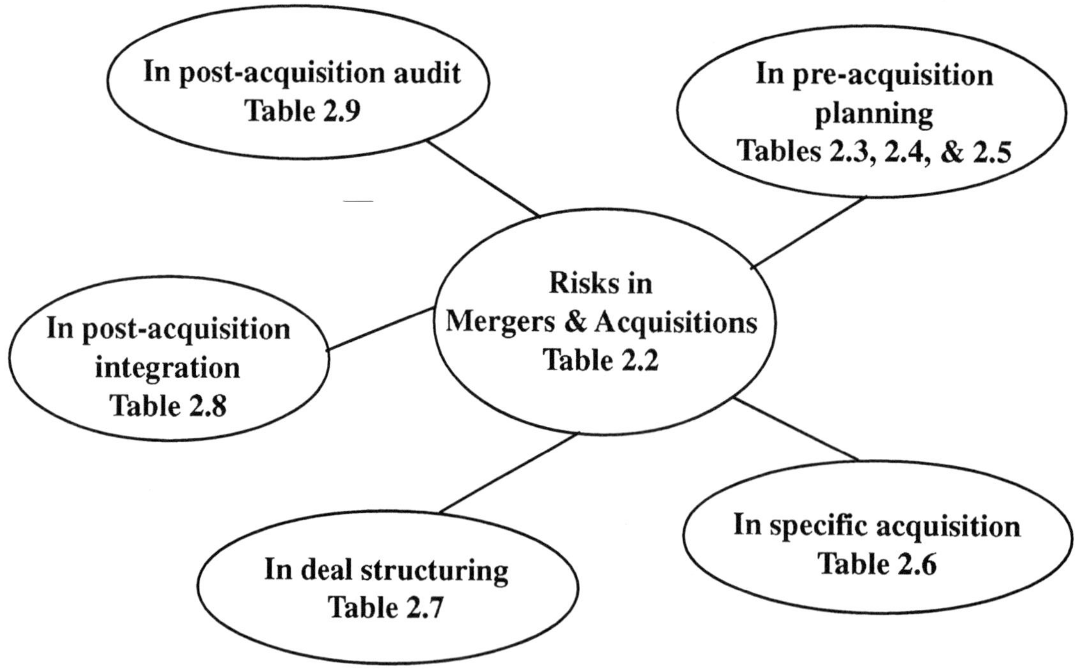

Figure 2.2
Strategic Planning — Stage 1

Figure 2.3
Specific Acquisition Planning — Stage 2

Figure 2.4
Deal Structuring and Negotiation — Stage 3

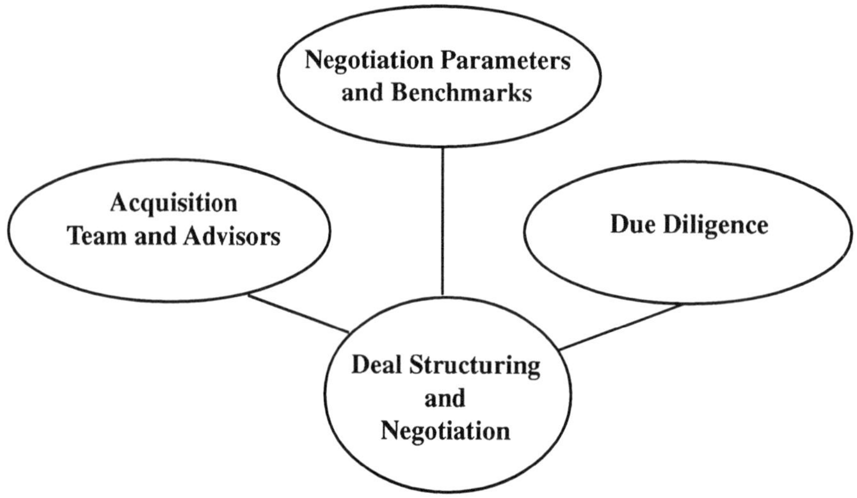

Figure 2.5
Post-acquisition Integration — Stage 4

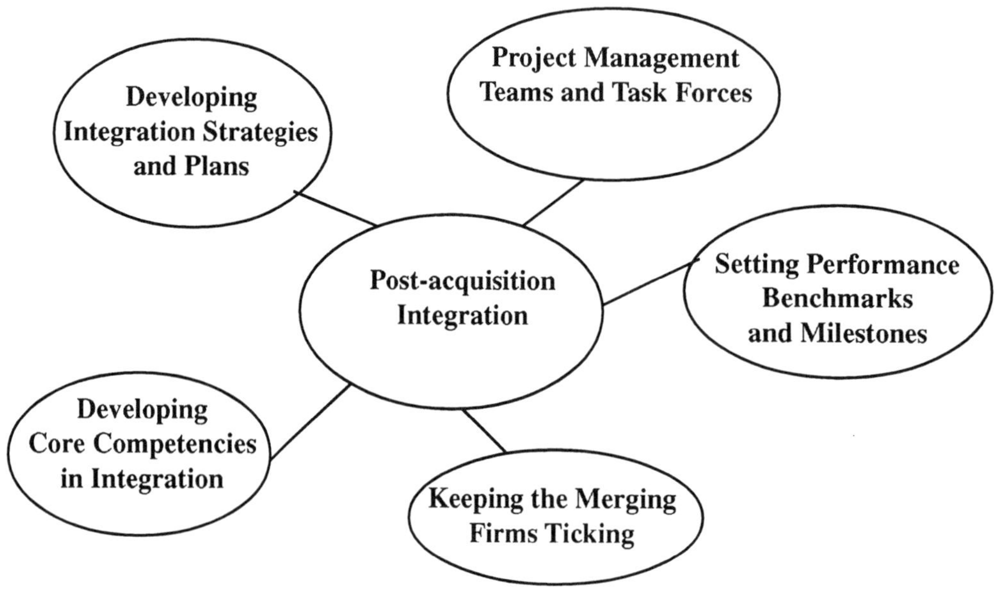

Figure 2.6
Post-acquisition Audit — Stage 5

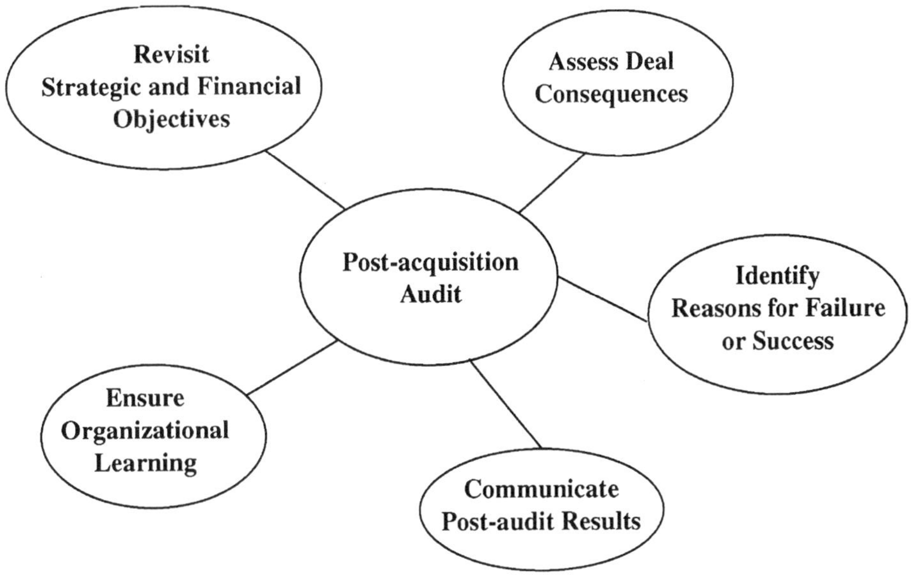

Table 2.2
Risks in M & A

- Mergers and acquisitions subject to a variety of risk causing the firm to miss its strategic, organizational, and financial objectives.
- These risks arise throughout all the stages of M & A process.
- The five stages in the M & A process are:
    - Pre-acquisition planning.
    - Planning a specific acquisition.
    - Deal structuring.
    - Post-acquisition integration.
    - Post-acquisition audit.

Table 2.3
Risks in Pre-acquisition Planning

- These risks arise from the processes and systems in place and hence organizational in nature.
- **Competitive strategy planning** — focus on company's overall competitive strategy as well as the competitive strategies of its business units.
- **Acquisition strategy planning** — focus on developing and evaluating acquisition strategies as an alternative to other modes of achieving the firm's competitive strategies.
- In both stages of strategy development flawed systems and processes lead to inappropriate competitive strategy and incorrect choice of acquisition.

Table 2.4
Risks in Competitive Strategy Planning

- Is the business model well developed and widely understood?
- Are the sources of the firm's current and future competitive strengths clearly identified?
- What is the mismatch between critical resources and capabilities available to firm and requirements of business model?
- How serious and how urgent is the mismatch?
- Can they be developed internally or do they need to be sourced externally?
- What are the alternative ways of assessing the resources/capabilities?

Table 2.5
Risks in Acquisition Strategy Planning

- What is the place of M & A in the firm's competitive strategy?
- Has a balanced evaluation of alternative modes of market entry and growth been made?
- What are the relative costs and benefits of these alternatives?
- How are M & A ideas generated?
- Are the relevant functions, business units, and the top management all involved?
- Is it one person, CEO show?
- Is there a robust pre-acquisition audit to say, "Emperor has no clothes"?
- What growth opportunities will M & A bring? Have they been mapped carefully?
- Does the acquisition program contribute toward converting firm's vision and strategy into operating results?
- Does the firm have internal acquisition deal making, integration, and post-audit capabilities?
- Does it have models of acquisition value, risk appraisal, and management?
- Does the firm have a good corporate memory of past acquisition successes and failures informing current acquisition program?
- Does the firm recognize acquisition function as an important capability, competitive advantage, and source of value?
- Has it devoted enough resources to strengthen this function?
- Is the acquisition function benchmarked against the best?

Table 2.6
Risks in Specific Acquisitions

Risk arise in:

- **Target selection**
  - What is the target selection process? Proactive or opportunistic?
  - Does the target match the acquisition criteria and desirable profile?
- **Strategic evaluation** of target
  - Missing synergy opportunities
  - Over-hyping intangibles and real options
  - Ignoring negative impact on acquirer's strategic assets
  - Ignoring cost of sharing activities
- Assessing shareholder **value creation logic**
  - Have the sources of value been identified correctly?
  - Are the correct value models used?
  - Does cost capital allow for increased risk?
  - Are the right benchmarks used in valuation using multiples?
  - Are the costs of realizing value correctly foreseen and estimated?
  - What is the time scale for realizing value gains?
  - Are the acquisition benefits inflated by sponsors' enthusiasm or vested interest?
  - Are due diligence results incorporated into valuation and risk appraisal?

Table 2.7
Risks in Deal Structuring and Negotiation

These risks cover:

- Selection of inappropriate acquisition team and advisers.
- Setting unrealistic negotiation parameters and benchmarks.
- Inadequate due diligence.
- Inappropriate and costly bid strategies and tactics.
- Not factoring in potential showstoppers and delays.
- Regulatory risk of prolonged delay, unbundling acquisition.
- Deals generate their own momentum leading to overpayment or ignoring risk.
- Real of deal being driven by preferences of external advisers.
- Risk of conflicting interests with advisers.
- Are the adviser compensation contracts designed to avoid perverse incentives?
- Risk of competing bidders driving up target premium.
- Are the antitrust, stock exchange, Takeover Panel, insider-trading rules observed?
- What is the mechanism for ensuring compliance?
- Are the directors aware of these rules and their fiduciary responsibilities?
- Are alternative payments carefully evaluated?
- In structuring payment method how is risk controlled? Use of derivatives?
- Does accounting rule preference drive the payment method rather than strategic or risk consideration?
- Does due diligence cover commercial, HR, environmental risks?

Table 2.8
Risks in Post-acquisition Integration

Risks in this process cover:

- Lack of integration strategy or plan to achieve the strategic and financial goals.
- Lack of project management approach.
- Absence of performance benchmarks and milestones for evaluating integration progress.
- Forgetting how integration distracts the firm from its normal business activities, i.e., taking the eye of the ball while integrating.
- Does the integration experience contribute to organizational learning and developing a core competence?
- Does the integration plan take into account the strategic and value creation logic?
- Do performance benchmarks reflect these?
- Does the integration plan cover all relevant aspects of the two firms
    - Organizational restructuring.
    - Cultural integration.
    - IT systems.
    - HR, remuneration packages.
    - Operations, production.
- Does the firm have a well-defined project management approach and project management capabilities?
- Is project management team adequately resourced?
- Does project management team provide continuity from acquisition team to completion?
- Do project management teams include managers from both firms?
- Does the integration process include effective communication strategies for internal and external stakeholders?
- Risk of key personnel deserting? "Beware of poachers."
- Does the integration process paralyse the normal business of the merging firms?
- Do they keep their market, customer, and supplier focus?
- What are the performance benchmarks and criteria?
- Is the timetable for integration overambitious?
- Does the integration plan allow for mid-course correction?
- Does the integration process draw on the corporate memory of past successes and failures?
- Does the process provide for feedback loop among strategy, acquisition, deal making, and integration to create an interconnected M & A program?

Table 2.9
Risks in Post-acquisition Audit

Risks cover:

- Absence of acquisition specific and thorough audit.
- Inadequate assessment of performance due to poor performance metrics or time scale for delivery of performance.
- Absence of clear identification of reasons for success or failure.
- Lack of effective communication strategies to communicate the lessons from acquisitions.
- Organization failing to learn due to absence of incentives for learning or fear of scapegoating.

- Have the deals been audited for delivering their promises?
- Separate acquisition audit or part of the normal internal audit? or
- Does the audit ensure appropriate benchmarks for type of acquisition made?
- Do performance benchmarks represent a balanced scorecard covering
    - Short-term and long-term objectives?
    - Financial, business process, and organizational learning objectives driving the acquisitions?
- Does the audit create a well-calibrated feedback mechanism for organizational learning?
- Does it facilitate single loop learning, i.e., understand reasons for failure of expectations?
- Does it facilitate double-loop learning, i.e., question the assumptions underlying acquisition strategy and program and its expectations?
- Are both successes and failures in acquisitions communicated effectively so they become embedded in organizational procedures, systems, cultures, and routines?
- Does post-audit lead to more effective acquisition process and organizational capability that confers a competitive advantage?

CHAPTER 3
RESULTS OF FIELD INTERVIEWS

Introduction

The researchers developed a research model to serve as an overall framework for the study. The overall research model is shown below. The literature review in Chapter 2 provided the conceptual basis derived from an extensive survey of extant research in the areas of M, A, & D. This also allowed the researchers to draw up an aide-memoire, which provided a comprehensive and standardized set of questions and discussion points for use in conducting the field interviews.

Figure 3.1
M, A, & D Research Model

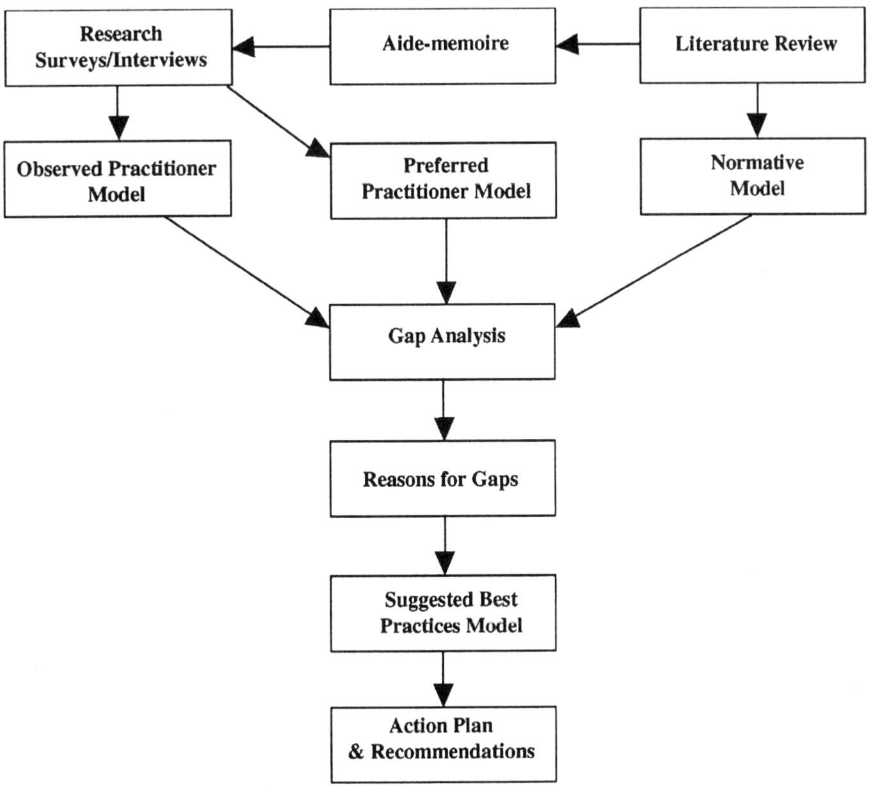

As discussed fully in Appendix II, the purpose of the interviews was to build up a "rich picture" of the actual M & A policies and practices of the interviewee companies, and of the role that internal audit played in this context. The researchers also made use of publicly available information (e.g., news releases, trade journal and newspaper articles) about the nature and type of recent M & A activities that the interviewed companies had participated in over the past few years. This was highly valuable since it provided significant specific deal information (i.e., time frame, costs, and justification for deals) and some commentary about the organizations' apparent business strategy driving deals.

The Macro Model in Figure 3.2 shows the various stages of mergers, acquisitions, and divestitures and how they direct the focus of the organization. Some stages focus on organizational processes and systems while others are focused on the transactional aspects.

Figure 3.2
M, A, & D Macro Model

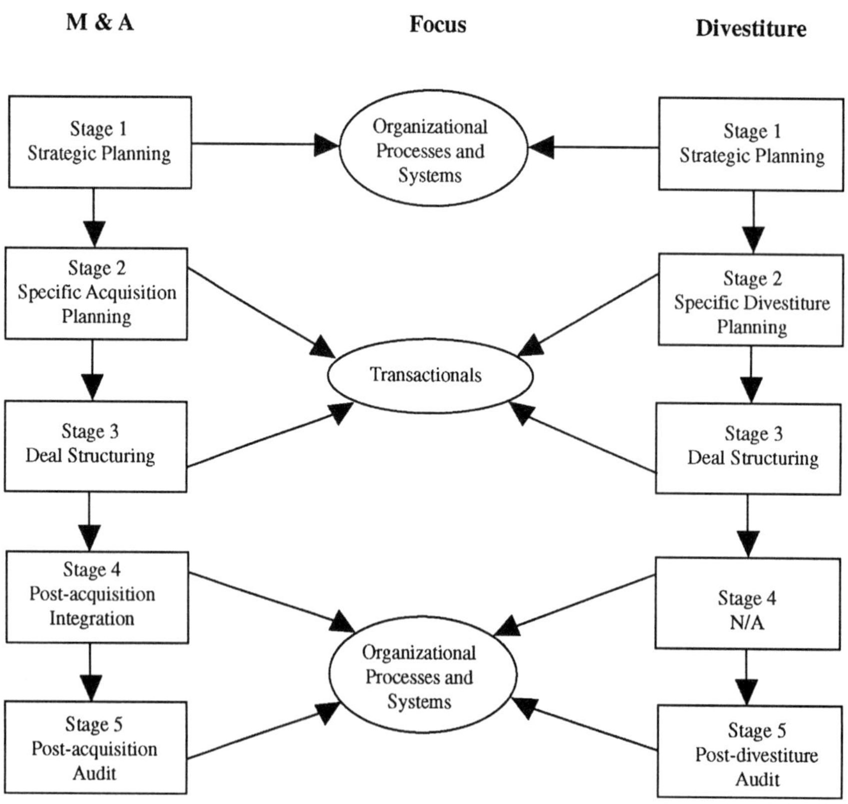

During the interviews, we ascertained the views about the future potential of internal audit's interfaces with the M, A, & D functions in the companies from those working in functional areas such as corporate strategy, information systems, finance, and internal audit. The information gleaned from both the literature and the interviews was used to construct the preliminary empirical or observed research model(s), which were then to be validated at the second stage. We present the information from the interviews as follows:

- The current roles and responsibilities of internal auditors in the five stages of mergers, acquisitions, and divestitures: strategic planning, specific acquisition planning, deal structuring and negotiation, post-acquisition integration, and post-acquisition audit,
- Summary of the internal auditors' preferred roles and responsibilities at each stage,
- The prerequisites of internal auditors to participate effectively in M, A, & D processes, and
- Means of achieving these prerequisites.

The researchers analyzed the individual findings in order to develop recommendations for best practices for internal auditors. The best practices define the scope of the opportunities for internal audit to increase its participation in these activities and thereby make an improved contribution to the organizations they serve.

An Overview of Participating Organizations

The researchers carried out interviews in 22 companies in the U.S. and Europe. In Stage 1, information collected includes details about the ranges of the IA staff sizes and the number of functions interviewed. First, the range of IA size is eight to 488. Second, the number of functions interviewed at the above noted companies is one to five. The diversity of staff sizes provided additional insights about the responsibilities of the internal audit departments and the nature of the auditing activities (financial, operational, IT, etc.) in their respective organizations. In Stage 2, limited demographic information was gathered about the participating organizations. No other information about the organizations or their internal audit function(s) was requested.

Actual Participation by Internal Audit in the Different Stages of Mergers and Acquisitions — The Observed Practitioner Model

The nature and extent of internal audit involvement in M & A activities differs considerably across our sample firms. In fact, the actual role played by internal audit in the different stages of M & A also varies. The following table summarizes the responses given to the researchers regarding the *actual role* played by internal audit in M & A activities:

Table 3.1
Summary of Internal Audit's Actual Participation in the Different Stages of M & A

M & A Stage	Nature/Extent of Involvement
(i) Strategic planning	• Audit the process used to develop business case. • Audit the process to see how risk is assessed and managed. • Audit the control process to investigate whether control issues were addressed in the planning process and/or planning and execution processes. • Develop a notional planning model. • Risk assessment of planning process. • Provide consulting services to develop guidelines. • Examine the business strategic plans.
(ii) Specific acquisition planning	• Review strategic implications and audit the business case for the acquisition. • Consult Corporate Strategy (CS) and advise on deal. • Receive communication about deals from CS. • Look at special projects, e.g., IT, to assess risk and provide internal consultancy. • Review the other company's control system. This should help ascertain whether or not their firm is buying a good business.
(iii) Deal structuring & negotiation	• Conduct due diligence (DD) with other functions such as finance, accounting, human resources (HR), law, pensions, environmental risk, etc. • Work with external consultants carrying out DD, if appropriate. • Ensure DD covers financial, operational, and compliance issues. • Carry out skills audit as part of IA's DD. • Manage outsourced DD audit. • Provide advice on contracts and accounting matters, e.g., consolidated accounts, if requested. • Audit risk assessment and IA function in target company. • In banking sector, DD involves financial valuation, loan provision, etc. • Provide independent validation of the assumptions used in pricing target. • Ensure people doing the valuation have the right qualifications. • Ensure weaknesses identified in DD are considered in finalizing deal.

Table 3.1 (Cont.)	
M & A Stage	**Nature/Extent of Involvement**
(iv) Post-acquisition integration	• Ensure regulatory requirements for internal control, e.g., in banking are incorporated into integration plans. • Assist in developing and implementing plans to integrate IA of merging firms. • Carry out gap analysis of acquired firm, i.e., gaps in risk and control systems. • Participate in integration project management teams or task forces with other functions. • Audit internal controls in the to-be-acquired company. • Review integration plans for internal control and IT systems. • Assist in acquired company restructuring. • Ensure the target is introduced to the acquirer policies and procedures. • Identify communication gaps between acquiring and acquired businesses and different levels of staff during transition. • Advise on risks, examine deal structuring and implementing to ensure risks taken into account. • Report on transition progress weekly, monthly or quarterly, etc. to the transition executive and, if necessary, the board of directors. • Agree timetables and benchmarks/key indicators for transition with operating units and audit progress against these. • Evaluate business stability during integration, i.e., maintaining normal business operations of the firms and keeping focus on the customers. • Ensure stability function has the necessary resources, e.g., hiring new staff or training existing staff. • Alert HR to key personnel retention problems. • Advise on project management issues during integration. • Audit financial reporting systems and consolidation of head office operations. • Audit acquired company profit performance before final closing of the contract term (one U.S. company).

Table 3.1 (Cont.)

M & A Stage	Nature/Extent of Involvement
(v) Post-acquisition audit	• Audit integration process to identify control weaknesses and to learn lessons. • Audit covers financial and operational controls. • Report findings to audit committee, board, business units, CS. • Use as benchmark the final business case for the acquisition. • Risk-based audit of policies, procedures, and controls in acquired company. • Assess performance against benchmarks, e.g., balance scorecard and action plans. • Identify need for post-acquisition appraisal by a business unit. • Audit the post-acquisition appraisal system. • Investigate whether the specific goals of the acquisition have been achieved, i.e., market share, profitability, etc. Work with M & A function. • Prepare "Lessons Learned" document about integration process. • Ensure company has a clear hands-on integration activity. • Develop standards and checklists for the governance of stand-alone acquired subsidiaries.

It is noteworthy that in one U.S. company, IA only carries out "small target" due diligence. In another U.S. company, IA is involved only when operational problems arise and is invited to help. In another U.S. company, no formal process for involvement exists, but IA is invited to contribute in some M & A deals.

In summary, the stages, in the descending order of the degree of IA's involvement in M & A, are as follows:

- Post-acquisition integration
- Deal structuring and negotiation
- Post-acquisition audit (in acquisition-specific audit, ignoring normal audit that may cover the acquiring business unit)
- Strategic planning (in risk and systems evaluation rather than business strategy evaluation)
- Specific acquisition planning

To help explain the possible reasons for internal audit's *low to moderate* involvement in M & A. We offer a number of possible suggestions. These are categorized as external and internal contributing factors.

External Contributing Factors

External contributing factors are situational in nature and deal with how other business functions view IA involvement. These factors include:

1. The main responsibility for M, A, & D rests with other business functions, primarily: corporate strategy, finance, executive management, and business development.
2. Board, top management, and other functions not aware of IA's capabilities.
3. The executive reward-punishment system ensures the business unit managers are accountable for their unit performance. Hence no need for IA to follow the specific audit trail.
4. Other functions perceive IA as a mere faultfinding function and are reluctant to engage it as advisors.
5. Other functions unaware of the breadth of auditors' experience with past deals and therefore do not draw upon that "corporate memory."

Internal Contributing Factors

Internal contributing factors arise from the type, nature, and extent of internal audit's own processes and procedures. These include:

1. Lack of resources, e.g., IA function often very small.
2. Fear of diluting the control function regarded as the *raison d'être* of IA.
3. IA keeps a low profile and does not communicate its strengths to other functions or top management. Involvement may often arise from the experience, background, and networks of the individual IA personnel.
4. Lack of focus on what contribution IA can make. Its strength is not in advising on commercial decision making but ensuring establishment of proper systems, procedures, and controls for risk reduction at different stages.
5. Audit trail is lost once the acquired firm is integrated, and so acquisition specific audit is not feasible.

At interviews, after the actual role of internal audit in M, A, &D was discussed, interview participants were also asked about the preferred role for internal audit. The next section analyzes their responses.

The Internal Auditor's Preferred Role(s) in the Different Stages of M&A — The Preferred Practitioner Model

During the course of field interviews with each of the participating companies, the researchers inquired about the preferred role internal audit would like to play at the different stages of mergers and acquisitions. Given that many of the chief audit executives that contributed to this research study have rich organizational experience and in most cases deep organizational knowledge of M & A, the information on their preferred roles, summarized in Table 3.2, is a highly useful contribution of the research. It offers great insight based on various personal experiences of the participating internal auditors.

Table 3.2
Summary of the Roles Internal Audit Would Prefer to Play in the Different Stages of M & A

M & A Stage	Nature/Extent of Involvement
(i) Strategic planning	• Ensure that there is a coherent planning process. Do their firms have an acquiring process, a means of vetting targets and what the objectives are? • Advise on systems and processes that could reduce acquisition risk, if invited to do so.
(ii) Specific acquisition planning	• Audit the business processes of the target company. • Look at the assumptions underpinning model used to justify acquisitions/divestitures. • Review composition of acquisition team to ensure that it contains people who have the right attitude to deal making, analytical skills, and the right attitude to risk. • Investigate whether there is too much pressure on the team to do deals. • Provide unique advice on cross-border deals, e.g., about workers' councils in Germany.
(iii) Deal structuring & negotiation	• Conduct initial due diligence in assessing internal control as well as other areas of the target business. • Review and evaluate financial models used. • Ensure awareness of regulatory and other compliance matters. • In negotiations, do the negotiation teams have a clear "go/no-go" areas? Are they prepared to walk away from an unattractive deal?

Table 3.2 (Cont.)

M & A Stage	Nature/Extent of Involvement
(iii) Deal structuring & negotiation (Cont.)	• Is there a process to regulate the negotiation and deal-making stage? How good is the process? • IA can define its audit scope so as to include cultural audit of target firm. • IA can advise on the integration of financial, personnel, and organizational policies, and on developing these policies.
(iv) Post-acquisition integration	• In helping communication with acquired company staff regarding systems, procedures, risk control, etc. • IA can "size up" the acquired company to see how it is run. So IA should be involved up front. • Prepare a checklist of activities necessary to "actualize" expected value from the acquisition. • Play a consulting role to functions carrying out integration. • Advise on the approaches to issues such as HR in planning the transition.
(v) Post-acquisition audit	• IA can do more post-audit as part of change management initiatives and this role can be extended to post-audit of individual acquisitions. • IA can move to continuous monitoring as done during merger transitions rather than the periodic normal audit. • IA can audit the organizational learning process for the lessons learned from past acquisitions. • Ensure that learning is shared among different functions. • Where post-acquisition review is done by business units, IA can train unit managers in carrying out these reviews. • IA can audit specific acquisitions provided it can develop appropriate methodologies (one U.S. company).

The above analysis leads to three specific observations. First, only five IA departments in the sample see any expanded role in auditing the strategic planning. Second, six organizations perceive such an expanded role in the shape of specific acquisition planning. Third, in Stages 3 to 5, most IA departments saw possibilities for a more extended role beyond what they were already doing.

Actual Participation by Internal Audit in the Different Stages Associated with Divestitures — The Observed Practitioner Model

Internal audit organizations may also participate in the different stages of divestiture activities. For divestitures, there are four primary stages: strategic planning, specific divestiture planning, deal structuring and negotiation, and post-divestiture audit. Table 3.3 below summarizes the current roles IA plays at these different stages.

Table 3.3
Summary of Internal Audit's Actual Participation in the Different Stages Associated with Divestitures

Divestiture Stage	Nature/Extent of Involvement
(i) Strategic planning	• None
(ii) Specific divestiture planning	• As part of regular audit, flag up under-performing units as potential targets for divestiture.
(iii) Deal structuring & negotiation	• Carry out a closing audit. • Ensure no hidden liabilities remain with vendor. • Identify undervalued assets prior to divestiture to help in pricing the deal. • Carry out due diligence. • Help identify any intentional and unintentional errors before transaction is completed. • Determine net worth to help price the deal. • Advise on warranties and guarantees given by vendor. • Advise on structuring the deal. • Help identify targets for divestiture. • Help prepare prospectus for sale. • Ensure stability while divestiture is in progress.
(v) Post-divestiture audit	• None

It should be noted that post-divestiture integration is not applicable since integration of the sold entity is not necessary.

The analysis presented in the previous table leads to the following observations. First, in only eight companies does internal audit have any role to play in divestiture activities. This is a small percentage (e.g., 36%) of the total organizations taking part in the research study. The stages in the descending order of the degree of IA's involvement are deal structuring and negotiation and specific divestiture planning.

The Internal Auditor's Preferred Role(s) in the Different Stages of Divestitures — The Preferred Practitioner Model

During the course of field interviews with each participating company, the researchers inquired about the preferred role that internal audit would like to play at the different stages of divestitures. Unfortunately, little information in this area was obtained. The first possible reason for this is the low volume of divestiture activities in participating organizations. However, this seems unlikely since many of our sample firms were active in M & A. The second reason is the seemingly low involvement of IA with divesting activities in their respective organizations.

Table 3.4
Summary of the Roles Internal Audit Would Prefer to Play in the Different Stages Associated with Divestitures

Divestiture Stage	Nature/Extent of Involvement
(i) Strategic planning	• None
(ii) Specific divestiture planning	• Assess divestiture criteria and related benchmarks. • Assist with identifying potential buyers.
(iii) Deal structuring & negotiation	• Evaluate the organizational impact of the divestiture. • Assess tax and compliance implications of divestiture. • Assist in the development of alternative solutions.
(v) Post-divestiture audit	• Determine the new value of remaining holdings in post-divestiture era. • Evaluate the possible loss of critical firm capabilities. • Verify warranties and indemnifies as issued. • Assess future business opportunities between the divested business organization and the parent.

As indicated previously, post-divestiture integration is not applicable since integration of the sold entity is not necessary.

Gap Analysis

When comparing the Normative Model to the Observed and Preferred Practitioner Models for M & A activities, a number of apparent gaps have been identified. It is worth noting that the incremental preferred future role addresses those additional areas of IA involvement beyond their current role IA (e.g., what else IA can do).

Reasons for the Gaps in Merger and Acquisitions

In relation to merger and acquisition activities, the researchers would like to present the possible reasons for the gaps noted in the above analysis under three categories: general, management-related, and IA-related.

General

1. Throughout the research study, it was repeatedly indicated that organizations focused on making the acquisition deal happen and then at a later stage worrying about integration and control issues. This phenomenon has obviously contributed to the failure rate of M & A. Perhaps, if organizations recognized the need for strong and effective controls at the early stages of deal making, this would improve subsequent integration efforts and thereby mitigate failures.

2. In most organizations surveyed, the due diligence process was not formal or exhaustive. Time, data access, and other resource constraints appeared to influence this critical process. This limited the effectiveness of due diligence as a risk assessment process.

3. Different, perhaps competing functions in the organization might be striving for different, and often conflicting, goals in accomplishing mergers and acquisitions (e.g., the underlying competing objectives of senior management, operating management, and board of directors).

Management-related

1. Management did not always appear to use a formal method for valuing the target company from a shareholder value perspective. Often in these circumstances, a defensive or strategic, rather than value creating, approach was taken to assess the suitability of a target.

2. Two highly acquisitive organizations emphasized the human factors associated with mergers, acquisitions, and divestitures. Well-organized and formal training plans and

personnel retention schemes appear to be highly beneficial yet under-utilized in most interviewee companies.

IA-related

1. IA appears to be quite uninvolved in the strategic planning process. This appears to be due to the fact that while IA would like to be involved, other functions in the company feel that it is their responsibility and not IA's to develop and execute business strategic initiatives.

2. IA departments may have inherent limitations (flexibility, staff shortages, skill constraints, etc.) that do not allow them an opportunity to pursue these types of special projects. Furthermore, IADs might not be able to employ specialists if the regular audit work does not warrant recruitment of staff with those skills that might be used for M, A, & D work.

3. IA needs to be a proactive, strategically aligned part of the business. Its personnel and service offerings need to fit in the organizations' culture and overall.

Reasons for the Gaps in Divestitures

As with our previous discussion, we present the possible reasons for the gaps in divestitures under the same three headings, namely: general, management-related, and IA-related, as follows:

General

General reasons arise from the inherent nature of divestiture transactions and level of divestiture activity within the organization itself. Specifically:

1. The sample of interviewed firms is probably not very active divestors.
2. Divestitures are less complicated deals than acquisitions requiring less involvement by a wide range of functions such as IA.
3. In all likelihood, divestitures are less risky than acquisitions since it is *caveat emptor.* Vendors only retain residual risk in the form of warranties and indemnities. However, they may face business risk arising from the opportunity cost of not retaining the divested entity.
4. Other functions are unaware of the breadth of auditors' experience with past deals and therefore do not draw upon that "corporate memory."

Management-related

1. Responsibility rests with the business unit. Divestitures tend to be small relative to acquisitions and therefore may be handled by the business units themselves.
2. Top management, board of directors, and others may not be aware of internal audit's full capabilities.
3. The executive reward-punishment system ensures the business unit managers are accountable to their unit performance. Hence, no need for IA to follow the specific audit trail.
4. IA services may not be required because of the limited transaction risk perceived by management.

IA-related

1. Lack of necessary capabilities and skills within IA. Since many IA functions do not normally recruit extensively from other internal functional units, and, in some cases, internal auditors have no prior experience of working in other departments.
2. Internal audit functions are often small and therefore lack resources particularly for unscheduled audits and projects.
3. IA keeps a low profile and does not fully communicate its strengths to other functions and top management. Involvement only arises from the experience, background, and networks of the individual IA personnel.
4. Lack of focus on what contribution IA can make. Its strength is not in advising on commercial decision making but ensuring establishment of proper systems, procedures, and controls for risk reduction at the different stages of the divestiture activities.
5. Unlike in the case of acquisitions, specific audit of the divested unit is by definition not possible. The residual business unit, *sans* the divested unit, may be audited as part of the normal audit. However, it is possible to audit whether the residual unit is better off after the divestiture and also the divestiture processes, systems, and procedures.

The area of divestitures seems to indicate less total organizational and IA involvement than in mergers and acquisitions. While all of the companies interviewed were active acquirers, their lower level of participation in divestitures results in fewer issues and recommendations in this area.

CHAPTER 4
BEST PRACTICE RECOMMENDATIONS AND ACTION PLAN

Introduction

Using the findings of the field interviews discussed in the previous chapter, this research can now present a variety of opportunities for internal audit to respond to the needs of their organizations in a more proactive and assertive manner. Chapter 4 addresses the recommended activities for effective IA involvement in M, A, & D (e.g., best practices), an inventory of the prerequisites by which IA can deal with these activities, and finally an action plan to highlight the methods that can be utilized to develop and implement the necessary prerequisites.

Recommendations for Effective IA Involvement in Merger and Acquisition Activities

A number of specific recommendations related to IA participation in merger and acquisition activities have been developed. These items are segregated into functional sections according to the stages of the M, A, & D process outlined in Chapter 2.

- IA should play a greater role in the strategic planning stage by:
  - Making sure there is a well-defined and organized strategic planning process.
  - Advising on systems and processes that can mitigate acquisition risk.
  - Addressing the risk assessment process within the strategic planning process.
  - Assessing risks mitigation techniques and control mechanisms.

Nygaard (2002) also notes that at this stage, IA could also critique the project team formation and help ensure that the scopes of individual project support team are clearly defined.

- IA can assist the organization in the specific acquisition planning phase by:
  - Examining the business processes of target companies.
  - Making staff resources available for special projects and the organization's internal M&A SWAT team.
  - Providing unique advice in special circumstances such as regulatory compliance.
  - Reviewing the composition of the acquisition team for representation and diversity of talents.
  - Assessing the financial and other pressures on the acquisition team to make the deal.

  - Maintaining a line of communication with the acquisition team and executive management throughout the process.

Additional examples of IA activities at this stage include: a thorough assessment of the target companies' IA function (e.g., independence, staff qualifications, prior audit results and reports, etc.), a similar review of the organization's compliance and quality assurance functions, and gaining access to external audit and consultancy reports in order to highlight "weak spots" in the company (Nygaard, 2002).

- With regard to deal structuring and negotiation, IA can expand its role by:
  - Conducting internal control reviews during due diligence.
  - Ensuring due diligence covers all necessary functional areas.
  - Reviewing and evaluating financial models and projections used by management.
  - Recommending go/no-go parameters for individual deals.
  - Advising management on integration issues and specific suggestions.
  - Assessing the "cultural fit" of the target organization.

At the conclusion of this stage, it is important for IA to communicate the results of their work in both a comprehensive and very timely manner. Further suggestions are offered by Nygaard (2002), including: IA's review of other functional department's due diligence reports, provision of "open issues" for management's attention to prior deal closure, and financial assessment of accounting provisions and estimates (i.e., reserves, write-offs, cost savings opportunities, and integration costs).

- With activities in the post-acquisition integration stage, IA can serve the organization by:
  - Loaning out staff to assist with the integration.
  - Providing consulting services to aid the business functions leading the integration efforts.
  - Reviewing and monitoring high, medium, and tactical integration plans and results.

In order to assist management in executing their responsibilities, IA can also conduct various oversight reviews. Examples of these include: verification of transition plans and escalation processes, reviewing new corporate policies, standards, and procedures, ensuring the resolution of pre-close covenant conditions and other legal agreements, and participating in transition activities (Nygaard, 2002).

- IA has an opportunity to help the organization in the post-acquisition stage by:
  - Increasing the number and frequency of related audits.
  - Reviewing communication mechanisms for lessons learned and organizational knowledge management.

- Providing training to business unit managers that conduct post-acquisition reviews.
- Implementing continuous monitoring of key performance indicators.

In addition to the above noted recommendations, another set of recommendations related to divestiture activities has also been prepared.

Recommendations for Effective IA Involvement in Divestiture Activities

The low level of actual IA involvement in divestiture activities indicates that this is an area where IA does not appear to have much of a role to play. Even with this being the case, there are a few recommendations that can be offered for those internal audit departments that seek to be involved with divestitures.

Internal audit should:

- Continually review low-performing business units and offer practical operational suggestions for improvement, including divestiture.
- Evaluate the business strategy case and the shareholder value justification for the divestment decision.
- Scrutinize the deal for the aftereffects on the residual businesses, e.g., loss of key relationships with the divested component, alternative sources of services or inputs previously provided by the divested business and the relative costs of retention versus disposal.
- Examine the risk exposure that arises from the need to provide warranties and indemnities.
- Advise on the appropriateness of the valuation models used to support the divestiture decision, the minimum acceptable price, etc.
- Advise on the appropriateness of the consideration form received.
- Advise the operating units undergoing "de-integration" of the divested components.

Lastly, IA auditors should seek new ways to become active in this area. This is because the number of divestitures and related business transactions (i.e., de-mergers, spin-offs, etc.) are likely to rise in the future as organizations seek to refocus their business portfolios in an endeavor to increase shareholder value.

A More Effective Internal Audit Role in M, A, and D: A Suggested List of Prerequisites

This research has identified a number of findings that argue for an expansion of internal audit's role in mergers, acquisitions, and divestitures. Some prerequisites were indicated by the interviews held with non-IA functions. The others were gathered through discussions with internal audit representatives, when the researchers asked what types of knowledge, skill, and abilities would be required for IA to be successful in this area.

However, this expansion of internal audit's role can only be achieved if certain prerequisites for such a role are incorporated into the internal audit department's inventoried skill set and area(s) of responsibility. The following table lists these prerequisites. The means IA can use to achieve these prerequisites are discussed later in this chapter.

Table 4.1
Summary of the Prerequisites for an Expanded Role for Internal Audit in M, A, and D

Prerequisite

- Knowledge of the firm's businesses and general M & A concepts and best practices
- Knowledge of the firm's corporate and business strategies and business models
- Good understanding of the various sources of risks to which business units are exposed
- Business acumen and maturity
- Established track record of innovative risk management solutions
- Ability to see the "big picture" from an overall business and corporate perspective
- Experience of operating businesses
- Perceived objectivity and detachment
- Perceived as a source of authentic experience and knowledge with an established record of setting up, monitoring, and auditing systems, processes, and procedures
- Good facilitators
- Good communicators with high credibility as neutral communicators
- Good interpersonal skills
- Organizational culture that values IA's input as a monitor, adviser, and consultant
- Organizational culture that values and encourages openness and inter-functional co-operation
- Awareness of IA's capabilities and resources for a proactive role by top management, i.e., the board
- Recognition of the usefulness of IA's contribution to improved systems and processes and to risk management
- Strong support from the board for a more proactive role for IA
- Awareness of the resources and capabilities of IA to act as an adviser and internal consultant

The Desired Prerequisites

The desired prerequisites are interesting and intriguing from a variety of perspectives. A large number of issues could be identified to provide useful recommendations for individual chief audit executive and to the practitioner community as a whole. These issues are divided into three groups for further elaboration.

- The first set of requirements deals with the overall internal audit strategy taken by the organization. Clearly, a broad understanding of the business, its strategic business units, and the associated business strategies are critical. This provides a foundation for IA to comprehend the fundamental drivers of the organization and also can provide insight into the approach that management takes to risks and opportunities in the marketplace. An open organizational culture allows IA to act as a monitor, advisor, and consultant — three needed roles in a large, modern organization. Through this approach, IA can lay the foundation for providing proactive and cooperative services to management and the board of directors.

- The second set of prerequisites covers the body of knowledge that internal auditors should have. This includes a good understanding of the various sources of risks to which business units are exposed. IA should also have a solid business understanding and maturity. An established track record of innovative risk management solutions can prove valuable as well since management will often seek the advice of IA to help develop countermeasures against risks. Furthermore, the ability to see the "big picture" from an overall business and corporate perspective is also desired, as is the experience in the business operations areas. This point was made on multiple occasions and is based on the premise that if internal auditors have prior work experience in related business operations, then management (both top and operational) will value their opinions since they command authority and credibility. Lastly, IA will also benefit from a perception of objectivity and detachment, so that its recommendations and advice are treated as unbiased and impartial.

- The next set of prerequisites deals with the individual skills and capabilities of internal audit staff members. Good facilitation, communication, and other interpersonal skills appear to be useful in the M, A, & D process. All of the companies interviewed indicated that in a typical merger or acquisition, a team approach is taken whereby each team member is tasked with a discrete set of responsibilities. The researchers found that, especially during the due diligence process, management is in great need of information regarding internal control weaknesses, inaccurate financial reporting, personnel and information systems problems.

Best Practices Action Plan and Recommendations

Action Plan for Achieving the Prerequisites

A number of specific suggestions were made by the interviewees (internal auditors and others). These can assist internal audit in achieving the prerequisites previously noted in Table 4.1. Included in the summary table below is a description of each prerequisite action item.

Table 4.2
Summary of the Means of Achieving the Prerequisites

Number	Description
1.	Recruitment of staff with experience in operations such as finance and other functions into IA
2.	Organizational policy that encourages such rotation
3.	Organizational incentive policies that encourage secondment to IA of staff from other functions and does not impede career progression in their parent functions
4.	Rotation of staff among different functions to facilitate cross-functional migration and learning about the state-of-the art issues and models
5.	Training in professional and personal skills such as facilitating, communicating, negotiating, consulting, and interpersonal
6.	Prepare inventory of skills and techniques within IA and identify how these can be exploited by other functions
7.	Communicate ("evangelize") to other functions in a non-intrusive, non-threatening way about how IA's skills and tools would benefit them
8.	Run workshops and seminars on the value of IA's skills and tools to other functions
9.	Change IA's self-perception from mere watchdogs, monitors, and "nit-pickers" to facilitators, problem-solvers, and consultants
10.	Build trust with other functions
11.	Convince top management to allow IA to build up key resources for a proactive role
12.	Identify how these can be exploited by other functions

Additionally, in the combined Stages 3 and 4 the feedback received on these draft models indicated supports for the preliminary research results. The respondents as a whole concurred with the preliminary models in general and provided some useful feedback for the research team. First, the internal auditors indicated that their previous work in the area of M, A, & D has been quite limited. Second, two of the respondents indicated that IA in their organizations has been involved in the following areas: integration of business functions, procedural reviews, limited accounting support, and providing other assistance when requested. As one internal auditor mentioned, "We have tended to do the deal and then move on to the next one (even though) nearly all of acquisitions have run into great difficulty; particularly with systems, quality, and skill set of employees and insufficient oversight and management of the integration effort."

Furthermore, while internal audit has assisted on the "back end" of some projects in terms of cleanup, the replies seem to indicate that IA would prefer to play a more proactive role in this area. To this end, the internal auditors felt that management needs to be willing to allow IA to become involved early in the M, A, & D process and provide "an extra pair of hands" to help improve the overall effectiveness of the pursued business opportunity. While the significance of the replies is limited due to a very small second stage response rate, they nevertheless corroborate the fundamental soundness of the first stage — preliminary model.

In terms of the items related to the **knowledge base and strategic points** needed by internal auditors to be successful in the area of M, A, & D, the following was identified:

- IA can recruit more individuals from within the company, and specifically within areas normally involved in these activities (e.g., finance, IT, strategy, operations). Some companies in this study went to the extent of setting up rotation programs whereby new employees were offered (and in one U.S. company forced to accept) a rotation through IA as part of their training program.

We also noted that a few companies thought IA was such an excellent training program that organizational policy forced many or all internal auditors to seek other opportunities in the organization after an initial rotation or "tour of duty" in internal audit. In one highly acquisitive U.S. organization, IA has been invited to sit on the company's strategic steering committee in an observation capacity. This allows the chief audit executive to stay abreast of all new strategic development initiatives, including mergers, acquisitions, divestments, joint ventures, and other opportunities.

- Once a set of core skills is developed by the IA function these should be marketed throughout the organization, so that all stakeholders are aware of the full range of IA's capabilities. It may be worthwhile to take this to a certain level of "evangelism" where IA can hold open houses and/or publish materials that describe their capabilities, talents, and areas of specialization.

- Also, it was found to be valuable when internal auditors built positive, trustful relationships with senior and middle-level managers. Michael Cottrell, chief financial officer of Bon Secours Health System, states, "Internal auditors are my best and least expensive consultants."

In order to succeed with the requirements related to **the skills and capabilities** of the members of IA's staff, three key factors were discussed:

- External auditors with specialized skills can be used to train internal auditors in related areas (primarily due diligence).
- Other training schemes in facilitation, consultation, and communication techniques can prove useful with regard to skill development in these areas.
- The audit committee and top management need to allow IA to build up the key resources required to deliver the necessary services in a proactive manner.

Once these prerequisites are achieved by internal audit and then communicated to the various stakeholder groups such as senior management, board of directors, and operational managers in all areas involved in M, A, & D, internal audit can deploy the best practices and make a greater contribution to their organization.

CHAPTER 5
REVIEW OF THE RESEARCH PROJECT AND AREAS FOR FUTURE RESEARCH

Introduction

In this chapter the researchers compare the research objectives with what has been achieved. Further we conclude with the areas where future researchers may wish to explore.

Research Objectives and Their Attainment

The main objectives of the research were to:

1. Describe and understand the role internal audit currently plays in leading edge companies that actively pursue mergers, acquisitions, and divestitures.

2. Examine the relative contribution of internal audit to the three main stages of the M & A process.

3. Assess the contribution of internal audit to the three main stages of the M & A process in different modes of acquisitions (friendly versus hostile), and in different types of business combinations (for example, advertising agencies, financial services, knowledge-based high technology firms, and traditional manufacturing firms).

4. Develop a model(s) of the role of the internal audit function which would enhance its effectiveness in helping the firm achieve its strategic objectives through creating a sustainable competitive advantage and long-term shareholder value.

5. Identify the resource capabilities that will underpin the model(s) of internal audit.

6. Suggest methods for augmenting for organization-wide credibility and appreciation of the useful role internal audit can play in complementing and enhancing the other functions in the M & A process.

It is worth noting that strategic alliances were not addressed in this study.

The researchers are able to confirm that these research objectives were met.

The findings of the interviews point very clearly to the fact that internal audit in the majority of organisations taking part in this study is already playing a very positive and constructive role in mergers and acquisitions and to a lesser degree in divestitures. Further exploration of such a role highlighted a desire by internal audit to become more associated with these activities at an earlier stage in the process. As to divestitures, the small number of organizations where internal audit is involved in the different stages of this exercise should not be taken as a sign of internal audit disinterest of taking part in this exercise but as a reflection of a possible bias in the selection of the organizations taking part in the study, a bias emanating from the simple fact that these organizations are inactive in the domain of divestitures. (Objectives 1, 2, & 3)

In addition, models were developed and risk factors at the different stages of M & A were identified and presented. Models relating to M, A, & D and covering the normative (built using the literature review); the observed and the preferred (both based on the interviews) were compared and a gap analysis was performed. The gap analysis was used as the basis for the recommendations and the suggestions for enhancing the organization-wide credibility and appreciation of the useful role internal audit can play in complementing and enhancing the other functions in the M, A, & D process (Objectives 4, 5, & 6). The detailed discussions of the above are found in Chapter 4 with a summary presented in the Executive Summary.

Areas for Future Research

The researchers would like to highlight for future researchers areas where studies can be carried out, studies which would help shed more light into the role internal audit is and could play in the context of M, A, & D.

(i) Replace case studies with surveys using mail questionnaires

While the researchers argued in this report for the use of case studies in collecting the research data, the limitations in terms of the small number of participants could be overcome through the use of questionnaires.

(ii) Carry out a longitudinal study

In this case a number of organizations could be selected and the researchers will act as "non-participant observers" in observing and evaluating the role(s) played by internal auditors at the different stages of M, A, & D and over the whole duration of the process. The wealth of information generated could provide rich basis for a changed role for internal auditors in this process.

(iii) Repeat the study — after three years — using the same methodology

This would allow the profession to identify the progress, if any, which took place since the first study and should explain reasons for such results.

(iv) Replicate the research study in countries not covered in the present study as well as in the public sector

M, A, & D activities are universal. Organizations (public and private sector) in all major countries indulge in such activities and the exploration of internal audit's role is crucial if we are to identify ways where they can contribute positively to maximizing shareholder/stakeholder value.

APPENDIX I
GLOSSARY OF TERMS

Acquisition — purchase of assets, businesses, or controlling stake in a company.

Bid — offer to purchase the shares in a company.

Capabilities — the firm's organizational abilities to exploit its resources to achieve its objectives.

Core competence — the distinctive capabilities of a firm that it excels in and that gives it a current or potential competitive advantage.

Due diligence — audit of a firm's assets, liabilities, resources, and capabilities to assess the risk in acquiring that firm.

Friendly acquisition — acquisition of the controlling interest in a target company with the support or recommendation of its management.

Hostile acquisition — acquisition of controlling interest in a target company despite the resistance of the management of that company.

Hostile tender offer — a tender offer resisted by the management of the target company.

Indemnity — a contractual obligation provided by the vendor to the buyer to compensate the buyer in the event of any loss under specified circumstances. It is distinct from an indemnity.

Intangible asset — resources of a nonphysical nature owned or controlled by a firm. These include goodwill, patent, license, trademark, human resources, and organizational capabilities.

Merger — combination of two or more companies or businesses to form a single company or business entity.

Post-acquisition integration — integration of the operations, functions, resources, strategy, etc. of the acquirer and the target companies after acquisition.

Real option — the option to make investment in business assets to exploit future opportunities in markets for products or services. It is not an option to buy or sell financial assets like common or loan stock.

Resource-based competition — competitive strategy that seeks to exploit a firm's various resources and capabilities to gain competitive advantage.

Resources — the tangible and intangible assets of a firm, including financial, physical, organizational assets, and intellectual property.

Show stopper — any event or development that prevents a takeover bid from succeeding or raises the cost of the bid prohibitively.

Strategic group — group of companies whose members regard themselves as being in competition, based on their perception of the strategies and capabilities of the other members.

Sustainable competitive advantage — competitive position a firm can maintain over a long period of time in the face of attempts by its rivals to erode that advantage.

Takeover — acquisition of majority controlling stakes in a target company.

Target — the company for whose shares a bid is being made.

Tender offer — invitation to the shareholders of a target company to tender their shares in exchange for cash or a security offered by the bidder.

Walkaway price — the maximum price for an acquisition that a bidder can pay without incurring a potential loss.

Warranty — a contractual representation that a particular statement or document is true. Given by the vendor to reduce the uncertainty faced by a buyer. Breach of warranty allows the buyer to claim damages from the vendor.

APPENDIX II
RESEARCH METHODOLOGY

Introduction

The purpose of this appendix is to explain the methodology and specific methods used in this research. Each of these areas is addressed in separate sections herein.

Investigators who seek to find the most appropriate ways of approaching research develop research methodologies. These are developed in response to the specific answers to questions such as:

- What is the purpose of the research? Is it to describe an existing phenomenon; is it to identify causal relationships, or is it to provide new insights?
- What control is the researcher able to exercise over the events associated with the subject of the research?
- What type of data is to be collected and what type of data analysis is to be carried out?

The following table summarizes the advantages and disadvantages of a number of research approaches, which may be used in formulating research design.

The research approach chosen by the researchers was the "case study approach." The difficulty associated with problems of generalization of the research results was partially overcome through increasing the number of organizations taking part in the study. This was preferred to other strategies such as surveys because of likely low responses rates (typically associated with mail questionnaires) and the difficulty of using such questionnaires to gain deep insight into issues associated with the role played by internal auditors in M, A, and D and their interrelationships.

The research design was developed on the premise that the researchers will carry out face-to-face interviews with individuals within each organization selected to take part in this research exercise. The different stages are encapsulated in the figures below and are fully discussed in the remainder of this appendix.

Table II.1
Advantages and Disadvantages of Different Research Approaches

Approach	Features and Strengths	Main Weaknesses
Laboratory Experiments	A small number of variables are subjected to testing of relationships and examined in a laboratory setting.	Experiments can only examine a limited number of variables from the real world where a multitude exist.
Field Experiments	Extends laboratory type experiments into real life, which creates a greater relationship to reality.	Identifying willing organizations to participate in this type of research.
Case Studies	Hopes to describe relationships, which exist in reality, but within a single or limited number of organizations. Useful in developing understanding reality in great detail and allows for an analysis of patterns.	Restriction on a few or even one organization, which in turn limits the generalizability of results.
Surveys	Gives snapshots of practices at a set point in time regarding relationships that exist in the past, present, and future. Allow a greater number of variables to be studied than in experimental approaches. Covers real work situations and are more appropriate to making generalizations.	Difficult to gain insight into the causes of phenomena being studied. Possible bias may exist in the respondent sample and/or population.

(See, for example: Saunders, M., et al., 1997, and Brewston, P. and Millward, L., 2001)

Figure II.1
M, A, & D Research Model

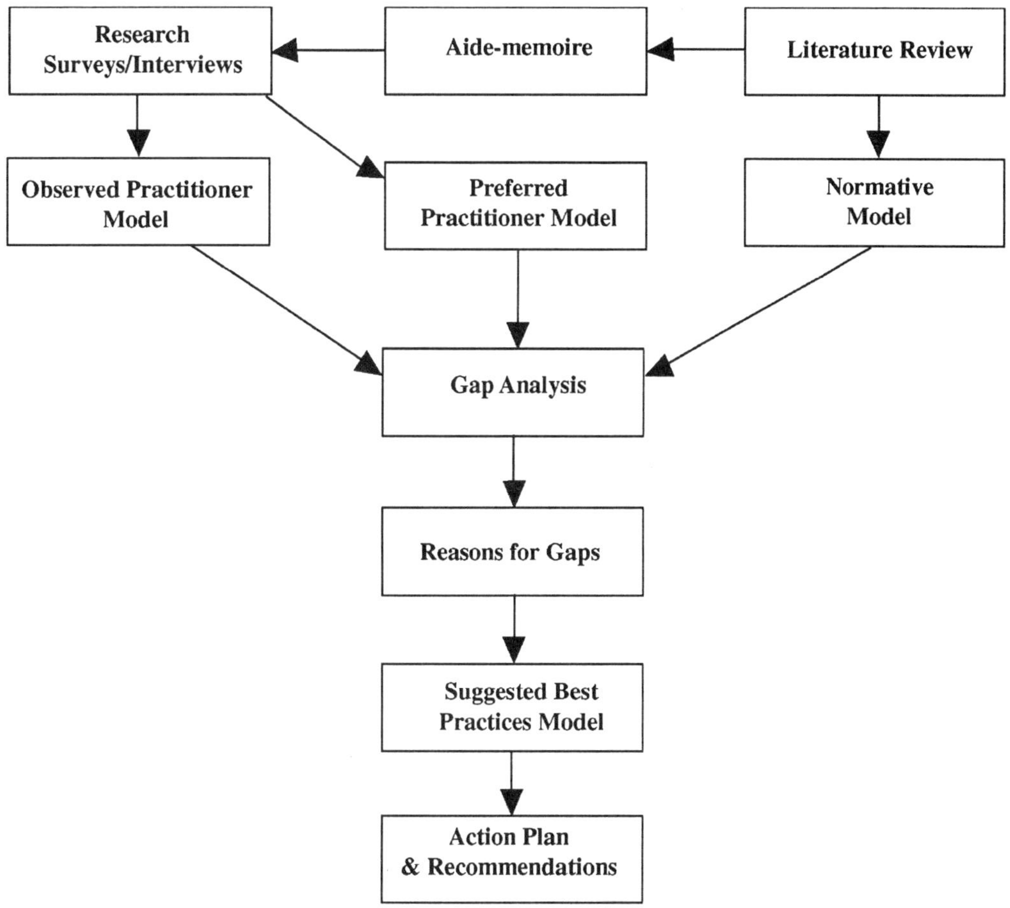

Figure II.2
M, A, & D Macro Model

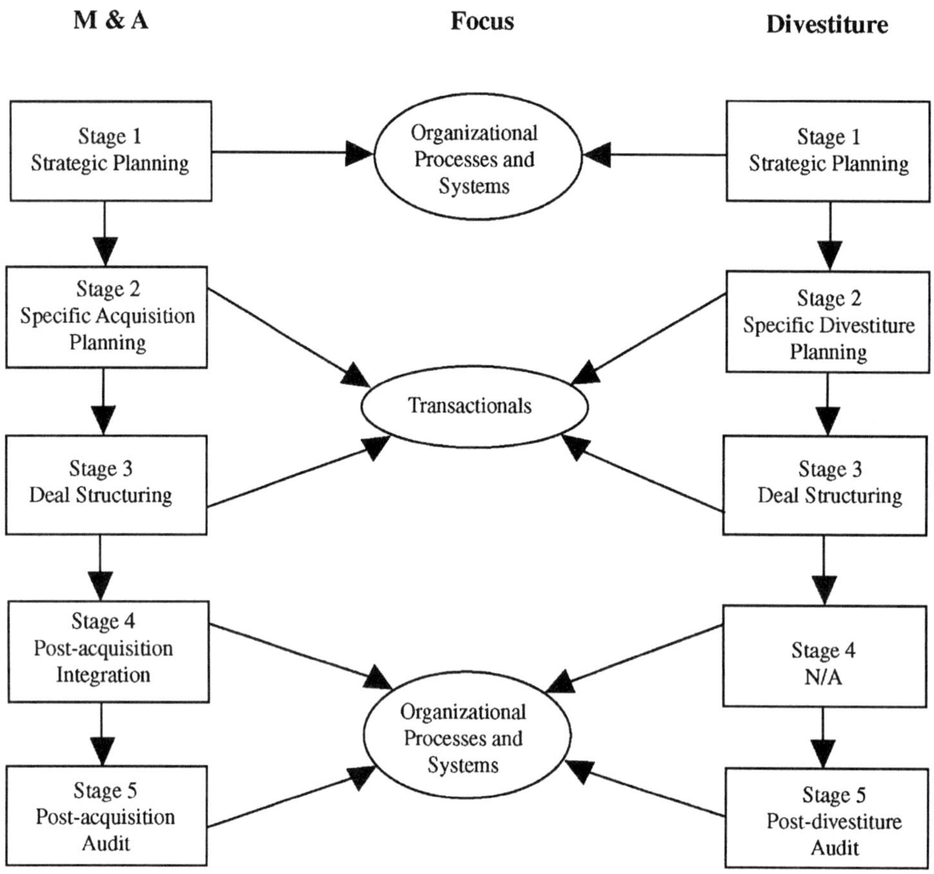

Stages of the Research

Stage 1: Preliminary Model Building and Development of Interview Schedule

- A comprehensive literature search of relevant published texts and journals was carried out. The literature search was aided by interrogations of electronic databases.
- Information collected from these sources was used as the basis for designing interview schedules.
- At the conclusion of this stage, the researchers had:
    - A preliminary and normative model for internal audit and its interface with functions such as corporate strategy, acquisition finance, etc., and
    - The criteria for the selection of leading edge companies where internal auditors had successfully implemented policies and practice which enhanced their role in the M & A process.
    - An "aide-memoire" consisting of a number of open-ended questions for use in carrying out the interviews (see Appendix III).

Stage 2: Case Study Interviews for the Development of the Model

The aim was to select a minimum of 25 organizations for this stage of the research work. The selected organizations would be drawn from manufacturing, banking and finance, knowledge-based industries, and IT. The researchers identified the different sectors, which are active in mergers, acquisitions, and divestitures by interrogating "Scientific Data Corporation" databases. Access to these databases was made available through the funding of The IIARF. The search provided the researchers with lists of potential interviewees in the U.S., Canada, and Europe (full details are provided in Tables II.2 and II.3). The geographical distribution would include U.S. and Canada (12), Australia (3), and Europe (10).

Table II.2
List of Potential Interviewee Acquirer Companies in the U.S. & Canada
(Cross-border acquisitions in bold)

Industry	Acquirer	Recent Target	Effective Date	Value $b
Financial Services	Nations Bank	Bank America	30.09.98	61.6
		Barnett Banks	09.01.98	9.1
		Boatmen's Bancshares	06.01.97	9.7
	Banc One	First Chicago NBD Corp	02.10.98	29.2
		First USA	27.06.97	7.3
	Travelers	Citicorp	08.10.98	72.6
		Salomon	28.11.97	8.9
	Chemical Banking	Chase Manhattan	31.03.96	10.4
	First Union Corp	Core State Financial Group	28.04.98	17.1
		First Fidelity Banc Corp	02.01.96	5.4
	American International Group	Sun America Inc	01.01.99	18.1
	Norwest Corp, Minneapolis	Wells Fargo Capital	02.11.98	34.4
	Washington Mutual	H F Ahmanson & Co	01.10.98	6.8
	Conseco Inc	Green Tree Financial Corp	30.06.98	7.4
Telecomm, Software, Internet	Lucent Technologies, Inc	Ascend Communications	24.06.98	21.4
	Nortel Networks Corp	Bay Networks, Inc	31.08.98	9.3
	Yahoo!, Inc	Broadcast Com	20.07.99	4.7
	Compaq Computer	Digital Equipment	11.06.98	9.1
	Worldcom	MCI Communications	14.09.98	42.0
		MFS Communications	31.12.96	13.6
	SBC Communications	Pacific Telesis Group	01.04.97	16.5
		Sothern New England	26.10.98	5.8
	Teleglobe	Excel Communications	10.11.98	6.4
	At Home Corp	Excite, Inc	28.05.99	5.9
	Cisco Systems, Inc	Stratacom, Inc	10.07.96	4.8
	Bell Atlantic	Nynex Corp	15.08.97	21.3
	BC Telecom (CAN)	Telus Corp (CAN)	31.01.99	3.1

Table II.2 (Cont.)

Industry	Acquirer	Recent Target	Effective Date	Value $b
Manufacturing & Mining	Halliburton Co	Dresser Ind, Inc	30.09.98	7.8
	Gillette	Duracell Intl, Inc	31.12.96	7.2
	James River Corp	Fort Howard Corp	13.08.97	5.7
	Sealed Air Corp	Grace Packaging (WR Grace)	31.03.98	4.9
	Raytheon Co	Hughes Aircraft	18.12.97	9.5
	Lockheed Martin Corp	Loral Corp	30.04.86	87.6
	Boeing*	McDonnell Douglas	01.08.97	13.4
	Rohm & Haas Co	Morton Intl, Inc	21.06.99	5.1
	International Paper Co*	Union Camp Corp	30.04.99	6.6
	3 Com Corp	US Robotics Corp	12.06.97	6.5
	General Dynamics	Gulfstream Aerospace	30.07.99	5.4
	Kimberly-Clark Corp	Scott Paper Co	12.12.95	6.8
	TRW (U.S)	**Lucas Verity (UK)**	**11.05.99**	**6.6**
	INCO Ltd (CAN)	Diamond Fields Res. (CAN)	21.08.96	3.3
	TransCanad Pipelines (CAN)	NOVA of Alberta (CAN)	02.07.98	4.9
Oil, Gas, Power, & Utilities	Exxon	Mobil	30.11.99	78.9
	Duke Power Co	Pan Energy Corp	18.06.97	7.7
	Texas Utilities (US)	**Energis (UK)**	**19.08.98**	**7.4**
Entertainment, Leisure, & Media	Walt Disney	Capital Cities/ABC	09.02.96	18.8
	US West Media	Continental Cablevision	15.11.96	11.4
	Westinghouse Electric Corp	Infinity Broadcasting Corp	31.12.96	4.7
	Seagram Ltd	MCA Inc	05.06.95	5.7
	Infinity Broadcasting	Outdoor Systems Inc	07.12.99	8.5
	Time – Warner	Turner Broadcasting System	10.10.96	6.9
	HSN, Inc	Universal Studios TV Assets	12.02.98	5.3
Retail & Hotels	Albertson's Inc	American Stores Co	24.06.99	11.9
	Kroger Co	Fred Meyer Inc	27.05.99	12.9
	Starwood Hotels & Resorts	ITT Corp	24.02.98	13.7
	CUC International Inc	HFS Inc	18.12.97	11.3
	Wal-Mart Stores (US)	**ASDA (UK)**	**20.08.99**	**10.8**
Services	Avis Rent a Car	Cendant Corp Fleet Mgt	30.06.99	5.0
	USA Waste Services Inc	Waste Management Inc	16.07.98	13.3
	Healtheon Corp	Web MD Inc	11.11.97	7.8
Drugs and Pharmaceuticals	**Upjohn (US)**	**Pharmacia (Sweden)**	**02.11.95**	**6.0**

Table II.3
List of Potential Interviewee Acquirer Companies in Europe

Industry	Acquirer	Acquirer Nation	Recent Target	Target Nation	Effective Date	Value $b
Financial Services	Fortis AG	BEL	Generale de Banque SA	BEL	29.06.98	12.3
	Kredietbank NV	BEL	Almanij-Banking & Insurance	BEL	11.06.98	7.6
	BNP	FRA	Paribas SA	FRA	06.08.99	13.2
	Axa SA	FRA	UAP	FRA	15.01.97	10.6
	AXA-UAP	FRA	Royal Belge SA	BEL	28.07.98	83.1
	Bayerische Vereinsbank AG	GER	Bayerische Hypotheken	GER	01.09.98	7
	Allianz AG	GER	AGF	FRA	12.05.98	5.1
	Credito Italiano SpA	ITA	Unicredito SpA	ITA	15.10.98	11
	Assicurazioni Generali SpA	ITA	INA	ITA	13.01.00	10.1
	Assicurazioni Generali SpA	ITA	Aachener und Muenchener	GER	09.07.98	5
	ING Groep NV	NL	Banque Bruxelles Lambert SA	BEL	19.12.97	4.5
	Banco de Santander SA	SPN	Banco Central Hispano-americano	SPN	15.04.99	11.3
	Banco de Santander SA	SPN	Banesto	SPN	06.04.98	4
	Nordbanken Holding AB	SWE	Merita Oy	FND	24.01.00	4.8
	Nordbanken (Venantius/ Sweden)	SWE	Merita Oy	FND	01.04.98	4.3
	Union Bank of Switzerland	SWI	Schweizerrischer Bankverein	SWI	29.06.98	23
	Credit Suisse Group	SWI	Winterthur Schweizerische	SWI	15.12.97	9.7
	Schweizerischer Bankverein	SWI	SG Warburg PLC-Inv Bkg Arm	UK	03.07.95	3.2
	Swiss Reinsurance Co	SWI	Mercantile and General Reinsurance	UK	06.12.96	2.7

Table II.3 (Cont.)

Industry	Acquirer	Acquirer	Recent Target Nation	Target	Effective Nation	Value $b Date
	Lloyds Bank PLC	UK	TSB Group PLC	UK	28.12.95	15.3
	Commercial Union PLC	UK	General Accident PLC	UK	02.06.98	11.2
	Prudential Corp PLC	UK	Scottish Amicable Life	UK	30.09.97	4
	Sun Alliance Group PLC	UK	Royal Assurance Holdings PLC	UK	19.07.96	3.8
	Prudential Corp PLC	UK	M & G Group PLC	UK	28.05.99	3
Telecomm, Software, Internet	Deutsche Telekom AG	GER	One 2 One	UK	01.10.99	13.6
	Ing C Olivetti & Co SpA	ITA	Telecom Italia SpA	ITA	21.05.99	34.8
	BellSouth GmbH (KPN, BellSouth)	NL	E-Plus Mobilfunk GmbH (Otelo)	GER	24.02.00	9.4
Mfg. & Mining	Coca-Cola Amatil Ltd	AU	Coca-Cola Bottlers Philippines	PNS	01.07.97	2.7
	Lafarge SA	FRA	Redland PLC	UK	31.12.97	3
	Thyssen AG	GER	Fried Krupp AG Hoesch-Krupp	GER	17.03.99	3.4
	Daimler-Benz	GER	Chrysler	USA	08.05.98	38.0
	Tabacalera SA	SPN	Seita	FRA	06.12.99	3
	Grand Metropolitan PLC	UK	Guinness PLC	UK	17.12.97	16
	British American Tobacco PLC	UK	Rothmans Intl BV (Richemont)	NL	07.06.99	7.5
	British American Tobacco PLC	UK	Imperial Tobacco Canada Ltd	CDN	01.02.00	7.1
	Siebe PLC	UK	BTR PLC	UK	04.02.99	6.1
	Reckitt & Colman PLC	UK	Benckiser NV	NL	03.12.99	3.1
	North West Water Group PLC	UK	Norweb PLC	UK	29.12.95	2.9

Table II.3 (Cont.)

Industry	Acquirer	Acquirer	Recent Target Nation	Target	Effective Nation	Value $b Date
Oil, Gas, Power, & Utilities	Electricite de France {EDF}	FRA	London Electricity (Entergy)	UK	04.12.98	3.2
	Scottish Hydro-Electric PLC	UK	Southern Electric PLC	UK	07.01.99	4.5
	PowerGen PLC	UK	East Midlands Electricity (DR)	UK	27.07.98	3.2
Retail & Hotels	Promodes	FRA	Casino Group	FRA	25.02.98	4
	Carrefour SA	FRA	Comptoirs Modernes SA	FRA	26.10.98	2.9
	Metro AG (Metro Holding AG)	GER	Metro Holding-Wrldwd WHL	DEN	15.11.98	2.8
	Metro AG (Metro Holding AG)	GER	Makro Holdings-European	UK	09.01.98	2.6
	Granada Group PLC	UK	Forte PLC	UK	06.02.96	5.5
	B&Q PLC (Kingfisher PLC)	UK	Castorama Dubois	FRA	18.12.98	4.1
	Great Universal Stores PLC	UK	Argos PLC	UK	07.05.98	3
	Bass PLC	UK	Saison Holdings BV	NL	27.03.98	3
Services	Cie Generale des Eaux SA	FRA	Havas SA	FRA	23.06.98	4.8
	Rentokil Group PLC(Sophus)	UK	BET PLC	UK	16.05.96	3
Drugs and Pharma-ceuticals	Sanofi SA (Societe Nationale)	FRA	Synthelabo SA (L'Oreal SA)	FRA	24.05.99	11.1
	Akzo Nobel NV	NL	Courtaulds PLC	UK	18.09.98	3
	Zeneca	UK	Astra	SWE	14.12.98	35.0
	Sandoz AG	SWI	Ciba-Geigy AG	SWI	17.12.96	30
	Glaxo Holdings PLC	UK	Wellcome PLC	UK	01.05.95	14.3

Within each organization selected, a minimum of four interviews would be held with different senior functional managers; (finance directors, heads of strategy, heads of acquisition function/team, heads of human resources and heads of IT/IS) plus the chief audit executive.

The key purpose of holding interviews was to build up a "rich picture" of M & A policies and practices developed and used in the companies, and the role that internal audit plays in this context. Views about the future potential of internal audit's interfaces with the M & A functions in the companies would also be collected. These would be used to build a small number of scenarios, which would support the next phase of the research. Information gleaned from both the literature and the interviews would be used to construct the research model(s), which would then be validated in subsequent stages.

The researchers were partially successful at carrying out Stage 2 as planned. As Table 3.2 shows, the researchers interviewed individuals in only 22 of the proposed 25 organizations. Also, we did not succeed in getting a minimum of four individuals in each organization. In addition, in spite of tremendous efforts by the researchers and the support of IIA Australia, we did not manage to interest three Australian organizations to take part in this study. Approaches to organizations inviting them to take part in the study started with a telephone call to the chief audit executive followed by formal correspondence (see examples of letter and attachments in Appendix III) identifying the areas of our research work and the people that we would like to have the opportunity of interviewing.

The following two tables show:

1. The distribution by geography and type the companies taking part in the research study **(Table II.4)**.
2. The companies and the interviewees taking part in the study **(Table II.5)**.

Table II.4
Companies Taking Part in the Study by Geography and Type

Sector	U.S.		Europe		Total	
	STAGE 2	STAGE 3	STAGE 2	STAGE 3	STAGE 2	STAGE 3
Manufacturing	2	1	5		7	1
Leisure	1		1		2	
Consulting			1		1	
Energy/Utilities	2	1	1		3	1
Real Estates	1				1	
Financial Services	2	1	2		4	1
IT/Telecomm	2		1		3	
Healthcare	1				1	
Total	11	3	11		22	3

Table II.5
Companies and Interviews Conducted as Part of Stage 2: Developing the Role IA Should Play in Mergers, Acquisitions, and Divestitures

The researchers carried out interviews in 22 companies in the U.S. and Europe. The following table briefly describes these companies in terms of their sector, the functions that took part in the study, and, where relevant, the sizes of the internal audit departments.

Company	Industry	Functions Interviewed	No. of Functions Interviewed	Size of IA (FTEs)
European Companies				
Akzo Nobel	Pharmaceuticals, chemicals, coating	IA	1	65
Argo Wiggins Appleton	Paper manufacturing	IA	1	15
AstraZeneca	Pharmaceuticals	IA	1	10
BAT	Tobacco	IA	1	125
Carlson Wagonslit	Travel	IA	1	14
KPMG	Accountancy and consulting	CO	1	N/A
Lattice Group	Gas distribution	IA	1	21
Lloyds TSB	Banking, mortgages, insurance	IA & RM	2	480
Daimler-Chrysler	Automobile, aerospace	IA	1	276
Olivetti	IT and communications	IA	1	169
UniCredito Italiano	Banking, asset management	IA	1	40
U.S. Companies				
Bank of America	Banking, financial services	IA, FIN, CS, Legal, FR	5	470
Bank One	Banking, financial services	IA, CS	2	160
Boeing	Aerospace, defense contractor	IA, IS, Network	3	110
Bon Secours Health System	Health care, hospital management	IA, HR, IS and FIN	4	24
Entergy	Electricity generation and distribution	IA	1	30
ExxonMobil	Integrated oil and gas	IA, FR	2	300
Lucent Technologies	IT & telecommunication	IA, CS, IS, HR	4	40
Microsoft	Software	IA, IS	3	19
Rouse Corporation	Real estate development and management	IA, CS, FIN, HR	4	8
Starwood	Hotel and hotel management	IA, FIN	2	30
Westinghouse	Construction, engineering, and manufacturing	IA	1	25
		Range 1:5	Range 8: 480	

Note: Key to abbreviations: IA = internal audit; RM = risk management; FIN = finance; CS = corporate strategy; FR = financial reporting; HR = human resources management; IS = information system CO = Consulting

Stage 3: Case Study Interviews for the Validation of the Model

The aim was to select a minimum of another 15 companies to help validate the model developed in Stage 2. The selection would be made from organizations based in North America (8), Australia (2), and Europe (5). Information collected from the interviews would be used to produce the validated model and the validated set of guidelines.

However, because of the difficulties faced by the researchers in finding the number of companies for carrying out Stage 2 as planned and in consultation with the project management team, it was decided to combine Stages 3 and 4 together and go to the world at large — through the Internet — to ask for comments and views regarding the research findings and proposals.

Stage 4: Model Validation & Statistical Analysis

The researchers planned to use the World Wide Web and the global reach of the Internet to place the key findings before the academic and practitioner communities for comment. We intended to validate the practical aspects of our model by encouraging some beta sites to develop, which the researchers will support through e-mail. The researchers would establish a Web site where the data could be placed for viewing and comment during the study period.

Combined Stages 3 and 4

The stages associated with developing and exploring case studies for the validation of the model and the World Wide Web consultation were combined for reasons explained above. Beginning in July 2001, the researchers summarized the research results to date and, with the assistance of The IIARF technical staff, displayed this information through The IIA Web site (http://gain2.org/mergers). In addition, the display included a short questionnaire asking for the reader's views regarding the:

- Research findings.
- Researchers' views regarding the role internal audit could play in the context of M, A, & D.
- Suggested prerequisites needed for such a role to be played by internal auditors.

Furthermore, the questionnaire asked whether the respondent was willing to take part in a telephone interview to last no more than 30 minutes. The full text of what was posted on the Web can be found in Appendix V.

The exposure through the World Wide Web yielded the following information:

- Number of hits: 381
- Number of respondents: 3
- Number of willing interviewees: None

The search for possible interviewees and contributors to this study has proved very disappointing. The researchers, however, are conscious of the considerable pressure that internal auditors and others are experiencing, which may explain their lack of commitment to this project. This occurred in spite of the support given by The IIARF.

Recording and Analyzing Data

Each interview obtained in Stage 2 was transcribed; some with the help of a tape recording used with the agreement of the interviewee. The different themes corresponding to the different stages of M, A, & D used in building up the "aide-memoire" were then used in recording and analyzing the interviewees' answers and views. This helped the researchers in the systematic analysis of the data. Furthermore, and wherever possible, two of the researchers jointly carried out the interviews. This ensured that better coverage and a fuller recording of the interviews was achieved.

Development and Validation of the Model

Data collected through the interviews were used in developing the models that describe the role that internal auditors *are* playing as well as the role they *could* play in mergers, acquisitions, and divestitures. The literature review provided a rich vein of information, which was used in building a normative model for internal auditors' role in such a context. Furthermore, the interviews with senior managers and internal auditors allowed a gap analysis to be performed and for subsequent recommendations to be made. The full analysis of data is provided in Chapters 4 and 5.

Summary

In this appendix, the researchers briefly described the research approach devised for investigating the internal audit role vis-a-vis M, A, & D. Difficulties experienced by the researchers in carrying out the study were discussed and the alternative research approaches that were adopted were detailed.

APPENDIX III
CONTENT OF COMMUNICATION WITH INTERVIEWEES

1. An invitation letter to take part in the study

2. How we are conducting our research

3. Aide-memoire for discussion with interviewees

An Invitation Letter to Take Part in the Study

September 2000

Dear (Interviewee):

RE: The role of the internal auditor in mergers, acquisitions, and divestitures

I am writing to ask for your help in the research work which Sudi Sudarsanam, Professor of Finance and Management Control at Cranfield University, UK, Rob Melville, Lecturer in Internal Auditing at the City University Business School, London, UK, and myself are carrying out. The research is funded by The Institute of Internal Auditors Research Foundation (IIARF).

For your perusal I am attaching:

- A brief overview of how we are conducting our research.
- A copy of the aide-memoire which the researchers are planning to use in the interviews.

Your organization has been chosen as an example of a leading edge organization, and we would like to include you in the study. I will be contacting you next week to explore the possibility of coming and interviewing you and several senior executives.

Thank you in advance for your help in this matter.

Yours sincerely,

Professor Georges Selim

How We are Conducting Our Research

The methodology is developed on the premise that the researchers will carry out face-to-face interviews with the individuals selected within each organization selected to take part in the research exercise.

Stage 1: Preliminary Fact Finding

A comprehensive literature search will be carried out of relevant published texts and journals. The literature search will be aided by interrogations of electronic databases.

Discussions with other acknowledged experts in the area. It is envisaged that extensive use of electronic media will be employed to trawl for opinions and views.

Information collected from the sources detailed above will be used as the basis for designing interview schedules for use when visiting organizations.

At the conclusion of this stage, the researchers would have: (i) a preliminary draft of a model for internal audit and its interface with corporate strategy, acquisition finance, etc. (ii) criteria for the selection of leading edge companies where internal auditors have successfully implemented policies and practices which enhanced their role in the M & A process.

Stage 2: Case Study Interviews for the Development of the Model

A minimum of 25 organizations is to be selected for this stage of the research work. The selected organizations will include manufacturing, banking and finance, knowledge-based industries, and IT. It is also envisaged that the geographical distribution will be: U.S. and Canada (12), Australia (3), and Europe (10).

Within each organization selected, a minimum of four interviews will be held with:

a) Different levels of management; (finance directors, heads of strategy, heads of acquisition function/team, heads of human resources and heads of IT/IS).

b) The chief audit executive.

The key purpose of holding interviews is to build up a "rich picture" of M & A policies and practices developed and used in the companies, and the role that internal audit plays in this context.

Views about the future potential of internal audit's interfaces with the M & A functions in the companies will be collected in these interviews. These will be developed into a small number of scenarios that will be used to support the next phase of the research

Information gleaned from the literature and from the interviews will be used to construct the research model(s), which we will need to validate.

Stage 3: Case Study Interviews for the Validation of the Model

A minimum of 15 (new and different) companies will be selected. The selection will be made from organizations based in North America (8), Australia (2), and Europe (5).

Information collected from the interviews will be used to produce the validated model and the validated set of guidelines.

Stage 4: Model Validation and Statistical Analysis

The researchers plan to use the World Wide Web and the global reach of the Internet to place the key findings before the academic and practitioner communities for comment. We intend to validate the practical aspects of our model by encouraging some beta sites to develop which the researchers will support through e-mail. The researchers will establish a Web site where the data can be placed for viewing and comment during the study period.

Stage 5: Follow-up Interviews

This stage will only be carried out if the results of the analysis of the data collected, after completing Stage 3, reveal contentious points which need further investigating before final recommendations are produced. These could be conducted as telephone interviews or through video conferencing.

Aide-memoire for Discussion with Interviewees

General

1. Do internal auditors have a role to play?

2. What is the scope of such role? Proactive or postmortem?

3. What is the role in the following specific areas:
   - Pre-acquisition strategic planning?
   - Deal structuring and negotiation?
   - Developing integration strategies and plans?
   - Implementing acquisition integration?
   - Project management?
   - Post-acquisition audit?

4. Do you envisage a more proactive role in the future?

5. What is the trigger for this change in perception of the future role of internal auditors? Failure of past acquisitions? Greater importance of due diligence? Need for internal consultants to evaluate acquisitions programs? Self-assertion by internal auditors? Need for internal auditors to justify their roles in their organizations? Reappraisal of the role of internal auditors by the profession?

Specific Questions

In Developing Competitive Strategy and Acquisition Strategy

What skills do internal auditors possess that can be of help to their firm in the following areas in the context of mergers and acquisitions:

1. In evaluating the firm's business model and the sources of its current and future competitive strengths?

2. In evaluating the mismatch between the firm's need for, and lack of, resources and capabilities for achieving its competitive strategic goals?

3. In evaluating the place of M & A in the broader corporate and business strategies of the firm?

4. In identifying potential growth opportunities through M & A?

5. In making a balanced evaluation of M & A and the alternative modes of market entry and growth such as organic growth, joint ventures, and strategic alliances?

6. In evaluating the comparative riskiness of the above alternative modes?

7. In identifying specific acquisition targets, target profiling, assessing target availability, and target vulnerability to a hostile bid?

8. In developing acquisition programs and strategies, evaluating the acquisition justification, the blueprint for acquisition-led strategies from the shareholder and long-term competitive advantage perspectives?

9. In evaluating acquisition programs within the balanced scorecard (BSC) framework and their contribution toward converting the firm's vision and strategy into operating results?

10. In coordinating the various functions within the firm involved in the broad acquisition program?

11. Developing the internal acquisition deal making, post-acquisition integration and value from acquisition capabilities?

12. In developing the necessary database on past acquisitions, their weaknesses and strengths, successes and failures, and in communicating the lessons from the past for future acquisitions?

13. Developing acquisition function as an important capability, competitive advantage, and source of value?

14. Developing models of value creation in acquisitions and in appraising the risk in acquisitions and consequences of that risk?

15. Evaluating the need for and choice of external advisers such as investment bankers, accountants, lawyers, strategy consultants, and environmental consultants?

16. Coordinating the efforts of internal acquisition team and the external advisers on a continual basis as part of the acquisition program?

In the Context of a Specific Acquisition

1. Evaluating the value creation potential of the proposed acquisition, taking into account the strategic logic, scope for cost efficiencies, revenue enhancement, synergies, post-acquisition integration problems, the risk of non-realization of expected benefits?

2. Evaluating the sources of added value — both tangible and intangible — broken down into assets already in place and real options?

3. How does the acquisition contribute to more effective internal business processes — innovation, operations, and post-sale service?

4. How does the acquisition contribute to more effective learning and the creation of new competencies that will enhance the firm's competitive advantages in future?

5. Making a realistic assessment of the time scale for the enhancement of business processes and organizational learning?

6. Assessing whether the acquirer and target firms have the organizational structures, systems, communication capabilities, and cultural framework for organizational learning where it drives the value creation logic of the acquisition?

7. Assessing the risk of failure in achieving the firm's strategic and financial objectives?

8. Testing the proposed acquisition against the shareholder value criterion?

9. Ensuring that expected benefits of the acquisition are not inflated by the optimism of the sponsoring manager and the cost of capital for the proposed acquisition adequately covers the risk?

10. Making sure assumptions beneath the value creation model are explicitly articulated and evaluated for realism and feasibility of accomplishment?

11. Simulating alternative scenarios for the outcome of the proposed acquisition so as to evaluate the attendant risk?

12. Incorporating the results of any due diligence of the target into the valuation and risk appraisal models?

13. Incorporating costs of externalities such as environmental costs, potential litigation, shareholder class action, etc.?

14. Ensuring deal negotiation, in particular pricing and bid premium, is carried out within agreed parameters and moderating the momentum of the deal so that negotiators abide by the parameters?

15. Ensuring that the deal is driven by the firm's strategic imperatives and not by the preferences of the external advisers by minimizing conflicts of interests between the firm and its advisers, e.g., investment banks?

16. Auditing the compensation contracts for external advisers such as investment banks to ensure no perverse incentives, e.g., high contingent fees for closing the deal no matter how high the bid premium? Such contracts may be partly driven by industry practice.

17. Ensuring compliance with the laws on anti-takeover amendments, insider trading laws, business judgment rules and fiduciary duties to shareholders, and directors' responsibilities?

In Structuring the M & A Deal

1. What is the role in evaluating alternative method of paying for the acquisition?

2. What is the role in assessing the accounting and tax implications of the deal?

3. What is the role in carrying out due diligence?

4. Does the internal audit function determine, influence, or monitor the due diligence carried out by outside professionals?

5. Is internal audit represented on the deal negotiation team? If so, what is the expected input and the scope of involvement?

In Post-acquisition Integration

1. What is the current role of internal auditors in carrying out post-acquisition integration of the acquired entity?

2. In developing appropriate integration models, taking into account the strategic and the value creation logic of the acquisition?

3. Role in assisting or coordinating the integration team?
4. In developing project management skills and capabilities in acquisition integration?
5. In preparing the merger integration plan and in its implementation?
6. What aspects of integration is the internal auditor involved in — organizational restructuring, cultural integration, communication, IT system integration, HR development, remuneration packages compatibility, operations integration, e.g., production, purchase, sales and marketing, R & D? What is the role of the internal auditor in integration of these areas and functions?
7. In developing the plan and timetable for integration and setting up benchmarks/milestones to measure progress?
8. In developing and implementing communication strategies and modes for internal and external stakeholders?
9. In coordinating the acquisition team and the integration team and improving communication between the two?
10. In ensuring retention of key players of both acquirer and the acquired firms?
11. In ensuring that integration process does not paralyze the operations of the merging firms?
12. In ensuring that the firms maintain their market focus?
13. In evaluating the progress and success of the integration effort?
14. In documenting and codifying the lessons from successful and failed integration efforts and communicating these?
15. In establishing the continual feedback loop among strategy, acquisition, deal making, and integration functions so as to create an interconnected M & A program?

In Post-acquisition Audit

1. In ensuring that performance benchmarks are appropriate for the type of acquisition made?

2. In ensuring that performance benchmarks represent a balanced scorecard encompassing short-term and long-term objectives, and financial, business process, and organizational learning objectives driving the acquisition?

3. In assessing the performance against the benchmarks?

4. Evaluating the reasons for the success or failure in achieving benchmark performance?

5. Developing a well-calibrated feedback mechanism to facilitate organizational learning?

6. Facilitating both single-loop learning, i.e., understanding the reasons for divergence between expectations and achievement and double-loop learning, i.e., using the single loop to question the assumptions and premises underlying the acquisition strategy and its expectations?

7. Communicating both successes and failures in acquisitions and ensuring that learning from acquisitions becomes embedded in organizational procedures, systems cultures, and routines?

8. Ensuring that post-audit leads to a more effective acquisition process and organizational capability that can confer a competitive advantage?

On Divestitures

1. What is the role of internal audit in divestitures?

2. In developing a program of divestitures, establishing the rationale as a shareholder value creating strategy, evaluating alternatives to divestiture?

3. In developing criteria for divestitures and benchmarks for successful divestitures?

4. In evaluating divisions and subsidiaries as potential candidates for divestiture?

5. In evaluating the organizational impact of divestitures?

6. In evaluating the impact on loss of critical capabilities of the firm and on its competitive advantage?

7. In due diligence of divestitures to assess residual risk and liabilities associated with the divested business?

8. In assessing the tax implications of divestitures and de-mergers?

9. In identifying potential buyers for the divested units?

10. In establishing the parameters for negotiation of price, form of payment, etc.?

11. In issuing warranties and indemnities?

12. In negotiating future structure of the relation between divested business and parent?

APPENDIX IV
EXTENSIVE LITERATURE REVIEW

Please go to http://www.theiia.org/iia/publications/bookstore/464_Appendix_4.pdf for a listing of the extensive literature review.

APPENDIX V
FULL TEXT OF M, A, & D WEB SITE

Mergers and Acquisitions

Welcome to our Web site and many thanks for your interest in finding out about the initial results of our research work. This research, ***A Research Study into the Role Played by Internal Audit in Mergers, Acquisitions, and Divestitures***, is funded by The IIARF and managed on behalf of the Foundation by a Project Management Team.

For more information about the project, link to:

Research team members

Research model and background information

This team seeks your views and your help in validating our findings and in contributing to the development of a practical model for an internal audit's role in mergers, acquisitions, and divestitures.

Please examine each of Tables 1 and 2 and then respond to the questions that follow.

Table 1
Summary of Roles IA Would Prefer to Play in Different Stage of M& A

M & A stage	Number of companies with IA involvement in activity (out of 22)	Nature/extent of involvement
(i) Strategic planning	• 5	• IA can ensure that there is a coherent planning process. Do their firms have an acquiring process, a means of vetting targets and what the objectives are? • If invited, IA can advise on systems and processes that could reduce acquisition risk.
(ii) Specific acquisition planning	• 6	• Audit the processes. • Look at the assumptions underpinning model used to justify acquisitions/divestments. • Review composition of acquisition team to ensure that it contains people who have the right attitude to deal making, analytical skills, and the right attitude to risk. • Investigate whether there is too much pressure on the team to do deals. • Provide unique advice on cross-border deals, e.g., about workers' councils in Germany.
(iii) Deal structuring & negotiation	• 15	• Initial due diligence in assessing internal control as well as other areas of the target business. • Review and evaluate financial models used. • Ensure awareness of regulatory and other compliance matters. • In negotiations, do the negotiation teams have a clear "go/no-go" area? Are they prepared to walk away from an unattractive deal? • Is there a process to regulate the negotiation and deal-making stage? How good is the process?

Table 1 (Cont.)

M & A stage	Number of companies with IA involvement in activity (out of 22)	Nature/extent of involvement
		• IA can define its audit scope so as to include cultural audit of target firm. • IA can advise on the integration of financial, personnel, and organizational policies, and on developing these policies.
(iv) Post-acquisition integration	• 16	• In helping communication with acquired company staff regarding systems, procedures, risk control, etc. • IA can size up acquired company, how it is run. So IA should be involved up front. • Prepare a checklist of activities necessary to "actualize" expected value from the acquisition. • Play a consulting role to functions carrying out integration. • IA can advise on the approaches to issues such as HR in planning the transition.
(v) Post-acquisition audit	• 17	• IA can do more post-audit as part of change management initiatives and this role can be extended to post-audit of individual acquisitions. • IA can move to continuous monitoring as done during merger transitions rather than the periodic normal audit. • IA can audit the organizational learning process for the lessons learned from past acquisitions. • Ensure that learning is shared among different functions. • Where post-acquisition review is done by business units, IA can train unit managers in carrying out these reviews. • IA can audit specific acquisitions provided it can develop appropriate methodologies (one U.S. company).

Notes:
* Two companies (one European and one U.S.) did not comment on preferred role as regards Stages 2-4.

Based on the above analysis, the researchers would suggest that:

+++ Only five IA departments in the sample see any role in auditing the strategic planning and specific acquisition planning process.

+++ At the deal structuring stage, only one company in the U.S. delineated an elaborate potential role covering the deal negotiation process of the acquirer. In other firms IA's potential role was limited to due diligence of the target.

+++ In Stages 3 to 5, most IA departments did not see a more extended role beyond what they were already doing.

* Our interviews also covered the actual and preferred roles of IA in divestitures carried out by the sample firms. IA participation in these was far less frequent than in the case of mergers and acquisitions. Analysis of interview responses in relation to divestitures is presented in the Research Model & Background Information.

CONCLUSION:

The researchers would like to conclude this summary of findings by arguing that an expansion of internal audit's role can only be achieved if certain prerequisites for such an expanded role are present in the function providing internal audit services. The following table lists these prerequisites and the means IA can use to accomplish them.

Table 2
Prerequisites for an Expanded Role for IA in M, A, & D and the Means of Achieving Them

Prerequisites	Mean of achieving these prerequisites
• Knowledge of the firm's businesses. • Knowledge of the firm's corporate and business strategies and business models. • Good understanding of the various sources of risks to which business units are exposed. • Business acumen and maturity. • Established track record of innovative risk management solutions. • Ability to see the "big picture" from an overall business and corporate perspective. • Experience of operating businesses. • Perceived objectivity and detachment. • Perceived as a source of authentic experience and knowledge with an established record of setting up, monitoring, and auditing systems, processes, and procedures. • Good facilitators. • Good communicators with high credibility as neutral communicators. • Good interpersonal skills. • Organizational culture that values IA's input as a monitor, adviser, and consultant. • Organizational culture that values and encourages openness and inter-functional cooperation. • Awareness of IA's capabilities and resources for a proactive role by top management, i.e., the board. • Recognition of the usefulness of IA's contribution to improved systems and processes and to risk management. • Strong support from the board for a more proactive role for the IA. • Awareness of the resources and capabilities of IA to act as advisor and internal consultant.	• Recruitment of staff with experience of operations such as finance and other functions into IA. • Organizational policy that encourages such rotation. • Organizational incentive policies that encourage secondment to IA of staff from other functions and does not impede career progression in their parent functions. • Rotation of staff among different functions to facilitate cross-functional migration and learning about the state-of-the-art issues and models. • Training in professional and personal skills such as facilitating, communicating, negotiating, consulting, and interpersonal. • Prepare inventory of skills and techniques within IA has and identify how these can be exploited by other functions. • Communicate ("evangelize") to other functions in a non-intrusive, nonthreatening way how IA's skills and tools would benefit them. • Run workshops and seminars on the value of IA's skills and tools to other functions. • Change IA's self-perception from mere watchdogs, monitors, and nitpickers to facilitators, problem-solvers, and consultants. • Build trust with other functions. • Top management to allow IA to build up key resources for a proactive role.

A01. What is the primary industry of your organization?

- ❑ Agriculture, Mining, or Construction
- ❑ Banking/Financial
- ❑ Chemical/Drug
- ❑ Communications
- ❑ Educational Instructions
- ❑ Government
- ❑ Insurance
- ❑ Manufacturing
- ❑ Petroleum
- ❑ Wholesale/Retail
- ❑ Services
- ❑ Transportation
- ❑ Utilities - Gas/Electric

A02. What country is your organization located in?

(country)

B01. Advise whether you and your IA department's preferred role is consistent with the description of the preferred role in Table 1 indicating how and to what extent it is inconsistent.

- ❑ Yes
- ❑ No
- ❑ Don't Know

B02. Explain to what extent your department's preferred role is inconsistent with Table 1:

B03. Advise whether you agree with the prerequisites and the means of achieving them listed in Table 2:

- ❑ Agree
- ❑ Disagree
- ❑ Don't Know

B04. Indicate your reasons for your agreement/disagreement with question 3:

B05. Share with us your experiences in cases of mergers, acquisitions, and divestments where you and/or your internal audit department played a role, the interface with other functions, the organizational perception of IA's role, its strengths and limitations.

B06. In addition, where you feel that your knowledge and experience would be beneficial to our research and you would be willing to take part in a telephone interview (maximum 30 minutes), would you please give us your name and telephone number (including the exchange code):

Thank you for your assistance in taking part in this exercise.

This questionnaire was created by GAIN at The Institute of Internal Auditors using Perseus Survey Solutions.

BIBLIOGRAPHY

Afshar K.A., Taffler, R.J., and Sudarsanam, P.S. (1992). "The Effect of Corporate Divestments on Shareholder Wealth: The UK Experience," *Journal of Banking & Finance,* Volume 16, Issue 1, pp.115-136.

Aggarwal, R., and Navratil, F.J. (1991). "Planning a Successful Acquisitions Strategy: Some Guidelines," *Managerial Finance*, Volume 17, Issue Number 1, pp. 14-19.

Ahuja, G., and Katila, R. (2001). "Technological Acquisitions and the Innovation Performance of Acquiring Firms: A Longitudinal Study," *Strategic Management Journal*, Volume 22, Issue 3, pp. 197-220.

Allen, J.W. (1998). "Capital Markets and Corporate Structure: The Equity Carve-outs of Thermo Electron," *Journal of Financial Economics*, Volume 48, Issue Number 1, pp. 99-124.

Allen, J.W., Lummer, S.L., McConnell, J.J., and Reed, D.K. (1995). "Can Takeover Losses Explain Spin-off Gains?" *Journal of Financial & Quantitative Analysis*. Volume 30, Issue 4, pp. 465-485.

Altier, W.J. (Jan-Feb 1997). "A Method for Unearthing Likely Post-deal Snags," *Mergers & Acquisitions*, Volume 31, Issue 4, pp. 33-35.

Anand, J., and Singh, H. (Summer Special 1997). "Asset Redeployment, Acquisitions, and Corporate Strategy in Declining Industries," *Strategic Management Journal*, Volume 18, Special Issue, pp. 99-118.

Andelman, D.A. (June 1998). "Merging Across Borders," *American Management Association International*, Volume 86, Issue 6, pp.44-46.

Arthur Anderson. (1992). *The Valuation of Intangible Assets*, London: The Economist Intelligence Unit.

Anonymous. (August 1992). "Black Days for Accounting Firms," *Journal of Accountancy*, Volume 174, Issue 2, p. 105.

Anslinger, P.L., and Copeland, T.E. (1996). "Growth Through Acquisitions: A Fresh Look," *McKinsey Quarterly*, Issue 2, pp. 96-110.

Anslinger, P.L., Klepper, S.J., and Subramaniam, S. (1999). "Breaking Up is Good to Do," *McKinsey Quarterly*, Issue 1, pp. 16-27.

Anslinger, P., Carey, D., Fink, K., and Gagnon, C. (November 1997). "Equity Carve-outs: A New Spin on the Corporate Structure," *The McKinsey Quarterly*, Issue 1, pp.165-172.

Ashkenas, R.N., DeMonaco, L.J., and Francis, S.C. (Jan/Feb 1998). "Making the Deal Real: How GE Capital Integrates Acquisitions," *Harvard Business Review*, Volume 76, Issue 1, pp.165-178.

Asquith, P., Bruner, R.F., and Mullins, D.W. (1983). "The Gains to Bidding Firms from Merger," *Journal of Financial Economics*, Volume 11, Issue 1-4, pp.121-139.

Barnes, P.F. (July-Aug 1996). "A Real World Focus in Calculating Terminal Values," *Mergers & Acquisitions*, Volume 31, Issue 1, p. 24.

Baskerville, R. (2001). "Conducting Action Research: High Risk and High Reward in Theory and Practice," *In Trends in the Choice of Qualitative Methods. Ed. Trauth, E.M.*, pp. 192-217, Idea Group Publishing, Hershey, Pennsylvania.

Beatty, C.A. (Summer 1994). "Wanted: The Perfect Tiny Acquisition," *Business Quarterly*, Volume 58, Issue 4, p. 50.

Belkaoui, A., and Pavlik, E. (July/August 1992). "The Effects of Ownership Structure and Diversification Strategy on Performance," *Managerial & Decision Economics*, Volume 13, Issue 4, pp. 343-352.

Berger, P.G., and Ofek, E. (1995). "Diversification's Effect on Firm Value," *Journal of Financial Economics*, Volume 37, Issue 1, pp. 39-65.

Biederman, B.J. (Nov/Dec 1996). "Valuing Software Firms in an Era of Cheap Technology," *Mergers & Acquisitions*, Volume 31, Issue 3, pp. 23-25.

Bogdan, R., and Ksander, M. (1980). "Policy Data as a Social Process: A Qualitative Approach to Quantitative Data," *Human Organization*, Volume 39, Issue 4, pp. 302-309.

Bowers, H.M., and Miller, R.E. (Winter 1990). "Choice of Investment Banker and Shareholder Wealth of Firms Involved in Acquisitions," *Financial Management*, Volume 19, Issue 4, p. 34.

Bows, A. (October 1987). "The Role of Corporate Audit Committees," *Journal of Accountancy*, Volume 164, Issue 4, pp.152-153.

Bradley, J. (1993). "Methodological Issues and Practices in Qualitative Research," *Library Quarterly*, Volume 64, Issue 4, pp. 431-449.

Brown, D.T., and Ryngaert, M.D. (June 1991). "The Mode of Acquisition in Takeovers: Taxes and Asymmetric Information," *Journal of Finance*, Volume 46, Issue 2, pp. 653-670.

Brown, S.R., and Melamed, L.E. (1990). *Experimental Design and Analysis*. Sage Publications, Newbury Park, California.

Brush, T.H. (1996). "Predicted Change in Operational Synergy and Post-acquisition Performance of Acquired Businesses," *Strategic Management Journal*, Volume 17, Issue 1, pp.1-23.

Buck-Lew, M., Wardle, C.E., and Pliskin, N. (1992). "Accounting for Information Technology in Corporate Acquisitions," *Information & Management*, Volume 22, Issue 6, pp. 363-369.

Buck-Lew, M., and Pliskin, N. (Winter 1992). "Corporate Acquisitions in the 1990s: Paying Attention to Information Technology," *Journal of General Management*, Volume 18, Issue 2, pp. 69-88.

Buckley, A., and Tse, K. (June 1996). "Real Operation Options and Foreign Direct Investment," *European Management Journal*, Volume 14, Issue 3, pp. 304-313.

Canella, A.A. Jr., and Hambrick, D.C. (Summer 1993). "Effects of Executive Departures on the Performance of Acquired Firms," *Strategic Management Journal*, Volume 14, Special Issue, pp. 137-152.

Carey, D. (May/June 2000). "A CEO Roundtable on Making Mergers Succeed," *Harvard Business Review*, Volume 78, Issue 3, pp. 145-154 .

Chatterjee, S., and Lubatkin, M. (May/June 1990). "Corporate Mergers, Stockholder Diversification and Changes in Systematic Risk," *Strategic Management Journal*, Volume 11, Issue 4, pp. 255-268.

Choi, F.D.S., and Lee, C. (1996). "Merger Premia and National Differences in Accounting for Goodwill," *Journal of International Financial Management*, Volume 3, pp. 219-240.

Christie, A., and Zimmerman, J. (Oct. 1994). "Efficient and Opportunistic Choices of Accounting Procedures: Corporate Control Concepts," *The Accounting Review*, Volume 69, Issue 4, page 539.

Clarke, C.J., and Brennan, K. (April 1990). "Building Synergy in the Diversified Business," *Long Range Planning*, Volume 23, Issue 2, pp. 9-16.

Comment R., and Schwert, W. (Sept. 1995). "Poison or Placebo? Evidence on the Deterrence and Wealth Effects of Modern Anti-takeover Measures," *Journal of Financial Economics*, Volume 39, Issue 1, pp. 3-43.

Comment, R., and Schwert, G.W. (1997). Hostility in Takeovers: In the Eyes of the Beholder? Rochester. Working paper.

Cook, R. (1993). "Auditing Acquisitions: Part I – Implementing Acquisitions Strategies," *Managerial Auditing Journal*, Volume 8, Issue 1, p. 28.

Cooke, T., Gregory, A., and Pearson, B. (Spring 1994). "A UK Empirical Test of the Larson-Gonedes Exchange Ratio Model," *Accounting & Business Research*, Volume 24, Issue 94, pp. 133-147.

Cotter, J.F., and Zenner, M. (Feb. 1994). "How Managerial Wealth Affects the Tender Offer Process," *Journal of Financial Economics*, Volume 35, Issue 1, pp. 63-97.

Coxon, A.P.M. (1999). *Sorting Data: Collection and Analysis*. Sage Publications, Thousand Oaks, California.

Creswell, J.W. (1994). *Research Design: Qualitative & Quantitative Approaches*. Sage Publications, Thousand Oaks, California.

Creswell, J.W. (1998). *Qualitative Inquiry and Research Design: Choosing Among Five Traditions*. Sage Publications, Thousand Oaks, California.

Cusatis, P.J., Miles, J.A., and Woolridge, J.R. (June 1993). "Restructuring through Spinoffs: The Stock Marker Evidence," *Journal of Financial Economics*, Volume 33, Issue 3, pp. 293-311.

Daley, L., Mehrotra, V., and Sivakumar, R. (Aug. 1997). "Corporate Focus and Value Creation: Evidence from Spinoffs," *Journal of Financial Economics*, Volume 45, Issue 2, pp. 257-281.

Darnell, D.C. (Summer 1999). "How Nations Bank Learned to Manage People and Change in the Merger Integration Process," *Journal of Retail Banking Services*, Volume 21, Issue 2, pp. 1-5.

Datta, D.K., Pinches, G.E., and Narayanan, V.K. (Jan. 1992). "Factors Influencing Wealth Creation from Mergers & Acquisitions: A Meta-analysis," *Strategic Management Journal*, Volume 13, Issue 1, pp. 67-84.

Datta, D.K. (May 1991). "Organizational Fit and Post-Acquisition Performance: Effects of Post–acquisition Integration," *Strategic Management Journal*, Volume 12, Issue 4, pp. 281-297.

Datta, D.K., and Pulia, G. (1995). "Cross-border Acquisitions: An Examination of the Influence of Relatedness and Cultural Fit on Shareholder Value Creation in U.S. Acquiring Firms," *Management International Review*, Volume 35, Issue 4, p. 337.

Davidson, M. (Second Quarter 1997). "Avoid These 7 Deadly Myths," *Oil and Gas Investor*, p. 19.

Deloitte & Touche. (1997). *Perspectives on Risk for Board of Directors, Audit Committees & Management*, London.

Denis, D.K., and McConnell, J.J. (June 1986). "Corporate Merger and Security Returns," *Journal of Financial Economics*, Volume 16, Issue 2, pp. 143-187.

Derwenter, K.L. (March 1995). "Does the Market React Differently to Domestic and Foreign Takeover Announcements? Evidence from the U.S. Chemical and Retail Industries," *Journal of Financial Economics*, Volume 37, Issue 3, pp. 421-441.

Dess, G.G., Picken, J.C., and Janney, J.J. (Jan/Feb 1998). "Subtracting Value by Adding Businesses," *Business Horizons*, Volume 41, Issue 1, pp. 9-18.

Dickhout, R. (1997). "All I Ever Needed to Know About Change Management I Learned at Engineering School," *McKinsey Quarterly*, Issue 2, pp. 114-123.

Dierickx, I., and Koza, M. (Sep. 1991). "Information Asymmetries: How Not to Buy a Lemon in Negotiating Mergers and Acquisitions," *European Management Journal*, Volume 9, Issue 3, pp. 229-235.

Dodd, P. (1980). "Merger Proposals, Management Discretion and Shareholder Wealth," *Journal of Financial Economics*, Volume 8, Issue 2, pp. 105-137.

Donaldson, G. (July/Aug 1995). "A New Tool for Boards: The Strategic Audit," *Harvard Business Review*, Volume 73, Issue 4, pp. 99-107.

Dyckman, T.R., and Thomas, L.J. (1977). *Fundamental Statistics for Business and Economics*, Prentice Hall, Englewood Cliffs, New Jersey.

Eccles, R.G., Lanes, K.L., and Wilson, T.C. (Jul/Aug 1999). "Are You Paying Too Much for that Acquisition?," *Harvard Business Review*, Volume 77, Issue 4, pp. 136-146.

Eun, C.S., Kolodny, R., and Scheraga, C. (Nov. 1996). "Cross-border Acquisitions and Shareholder Wealth: Tests of the Synergy and Internalisation Hypotheses," *Journal of Banking and Finance*, Volume 20, Issue 9, pp. 1559-1582.

Flaster, M.L. (Sept. 1995). "Establishing a Value-Enhancing Mergers and Acquisitions Strategy," *Texas Banking*, Volume 85, Issue 9, p. 6.

Fowler, F.J. Jr. (1995). *Improving Survey Questions*. Sage Publications, London, England.

Franks, J., Harris, R., and Mayer, C. (1988). "Means of Payment on Takeovers: Results for the UK and the U.S." A Auerbach (Ed.) *Mergers & Acquisitions*, University of Chicago Press.

Franks, J., and Mayer, C. (Jan. 1996). "Hostile Takeovers and the Correction of Managerial Failure," *Journal of Financial Economics*, Volume 40, Issue 1, pp. 163-181.

Franks, J., and Mayer, C. (April 1990). "Hostile Takeovers and the Correction of Managerial Failure," *Journal of Financial Economic*, Volume 40, Issue 1, pp. 163-182.

Galpin, T.J., and Robinson, D.E. (Jan.-Feb. 1997). "Merger Integration: The Ultimate Change Management Challenge," *Mergers & Acquisitions*, Volume 31, Issue 4, pp. 24-28.

Gates, C.B. (Nov/Dec 1988). "Get the Most Value from Your Acquisition," *Journal of Business Strategy*, Volume 9, Issue 6, pp. 8-12.

Ghosh, A., and Ruland, W. (April 1998). "Managerial Ownership, the Method of Payment for Acquisitions and Executive Job Retention," *Journal of Finance*, Volume 53, Issue 2, pp. 785-798.

Ghosh, A. (2001), "Does Operating Performance Really Improve Following Corporate Acquisitions?," *Journal of Corporate Finance*, Volume 7, Issue 2, pp.151-178.

Giacomazzi, F., Panella, C., Pernici, B., and Sansoni, M. (Nov. 1997). "Information Systems Integration in M & A: A Normative Model," *Information and Management*, Volume 32, Issue 6, pp. 289-302.

Gibbons, J.D. (1993). *Nonparametric Statistics: An Introduction*, Sage Publications, Newbury Park, California.

Gilson, S., Healy, P., and Palepu, K., Corporate Focus and the Benefits from More Specialised Analyst Coverage, Harvard University Business School. Working Paper.

Goodwin, C. (July 1999). "Merging IT," *Accountancy*, Volume 124, Issue 1271, pp. 37-38.

Goold, M., Campbell, A., and Luchs, K. (Dec. 1993). "Strategies and Styles Revisited: 'Strategic Control' – Is it Tenable?" *Long Range Planning*, Volume 26, Issue 6, pp. 54-62.

Goold, M., Campbell, A., and Luchs, K. (1993). "Strategies and Styles Revisited: Strategic Planning and Financial Control," *Long Range Planning*, Volume 26, Issue 5, pp. 49-60.

Green, J.M. (Dec. 1992). "Structuring an Acquisition Strategy," *Small Business Reports*, Volume 17, Issue 12, pp. 50-58.

Green, J.C., and Caracelli, V.J. (1997). *Advances in Mixed Method Evaluation: The Challenges and Benefits of Integrating Diverse Paradigms*, Jossey-Bass Publishers, California, New Directions for Evaluation, Volume 74.

Gregory, A. (Sept. 1997). "An Examination of the Long Run Performance of UK Acquiring Firms," *Journal of Business Finance & Accounting*, Volume 24, Issue 7 & 8, pp. 971-1002.

Grundy, A. (Jun 1993). "Putting Value on Strategy," *Long Range Planning*, Volume 26, Issue 3, pp. 87-94.

Guedes, J., and Parayre, R. (Aug. 1997). "Managerial Reputation and Divisional Sell-offs: A Model and Empirical Test," *Journal of Banking & Finance*, Volume 21, Issue 8, pp. 1085-1106.

Gunther, S. (Feb. 1979). "The CPA's Role in Mergers and Acquisitions," *The Journal of Accountancy*, Volume 147, Issue 2, p. 47.

Habib, M.A., Johnsen, D.B., and Naik, N.Y. (1997). "Spin-offs and Information," *Journal of Financial Inter-mediation*, Volume 6, pp. 153-176.

Hamel, J., Dufour, S., and Fortin, D. (1993). *Case Study Methods*. Sage Publications, Newbury Park, California.

Haworth, R.G. (Jan./Feb. 1994). "A Bold New Day for M&A," *The Journal of Business Strategy*, Volume 15, Issue 1, p. 32.

Healy, P.M., Palepu, K.G., and Ruback, R.S. (April 1992). "Does, Corporate Performance Improve After Mergers?," *Journal of Financial Economics*, Volume 31, Issue 2, pp. 135-175.

Hennart, J., and Reddy, S. (Jan 1997). "The Choice Between Mergers/Acquisitions and Joint Ventures: The Case of Japanese Investors in the United States," *Strategic Management Journal*, Volume 18, Issue 1, pp. 1-12.

Higson, C., and Elliott, J. (1998). "Post-takeover Returns: The UK Evidence," *Journal of Empirical Finance*, Volume 5, Issue 1, pp. 27-46.

Hitt, M.A., Hoskisson, R.E., and Ireland, R.D. (Summer 1990). "Mergers and Acquisitions and Managerial Commitment to Innovation in M-Form Firms," *Strategic Management Journal*, Volume 11, Issue 29, pp. 29-47.

Hitt, M., Harrison, J., Ireland, R. Duane and Best, A. (1998). "Attributes of Successful and Unsuccessful Acquisitions of U.S. Firms," *British Journal of Management*, Volume 9, pp. 91-114.

Hitt, M.A., Hoskisson, R.E., and Kim, H. (Aug. 1997). "International Diversification: Effects on Innovation and Firm Performance in Product-diversified Firms," *Academy of Management Journal*, Volume 40, Issue 4, pp. 767-798.

Hoffman, T. (Dec. 23, 1996- Jan. 2, 1997). "Boeing Merger Faces IT Turbulence," *Computerworld*, Volume 30, Issue 52, pp.1, 124.

Holderness, C.G., and Sheehan, D.P. (Dec. 1985). "Raiders or Saviours? The Evidence on Six Controversial Investors," *Journal of Financial Economics*, Volume 14, Issue 4, pp. 555 –570.

Holl, P., and Kyriazis, D. (Sept. 1997). "Agency, Bid Resistance and the Market for Corporate Control," *Journal of Business Finance and Accounting*, Volume 24, Issue 7&8, pp. 1037-1066.

Hoskisson, R.O., and Johnson, R.A. (Nov. 1992). "Corporate Restructuring and Strategic Change: The Effect on Diversification Strategy and R & D Intensity," *Strategic Management Journal*, Volume 13, Issue 8, pp. 625-634.

Hulle, C. Van, Vermaelen, T., and Wouters, P. (1991). "Regulation, Taxes and the Market for Corporate Control in Belgium," *Journal of Banking & Finance*, Volume 15, pp. 1143-1170.

Jarrell, S.L. (1991). The Post-merger Performance of Corporate Takeovers, Emory University. Working Paper.

Jauch, L.R., Osborn, R.N., and Martin, T.N. (1980). "Structured Content Analysis of Cases: A Contemporary Method for Organizational Research," *Academy of Management Research*, Volume 5, Issue 4, pp. 517-525.

John, K., and Ofek, E. (Jan. 1995). "Asset Sales and Increase in Focus," *Journal of Financial Economics*, Volume 37, Issue 1, pp. 105-126.

Johnson, M.P. (June 1989). "Compatible Information Systems A Key to Merger Success," *Healthcare Financial Management*, Volume 43, Issue 6, pp. 56-59.

Johnson, R.A., and Wichern, D.W. (1988). *Applied Multivariate Statistical Analysis*. Second Edition, Prentice Hall, Englewood Cliffs, New Jersey.

Kaiser, K., and Stouraitis, A. (June 1995). "Value Creation Through Corporate Restructuring: European Divestitures," *European Management Journal*, Volume 13, Issue 2, pp. 164-174.

Kaiser, K.M.J., and Stouraitis, A. (June 1995). "Agency Costs and Strategic Considerations Behind Sell-offs: The UK Evidence," *European Financial Management*, Volume 13, Issue 2, pp. 164-175.

Kang, J-K. (Dec. 1993). "The International Market for Corporate Control: M & A of U.S. Firms by Japanese Firms," *Journal of Financial Economics*, Volume 34, Issue 3, pp. 345-371.

Kaplan, S.N., and Ruback, R. (Sept. 1995). "The Valuation of Cash Flow Forecasts: An Empirical Analysis," *Journal of Finance*, Volume 50, Issue 4, pp. 1059-183.

Katzenbach, J.R. (1996). "Real Change Leaders," *McKinsey Quarterly*, Issue 1, p. 148.

Kesner, I.F., Shapiro, D.L., and Sharma, A. (1994). "Brokering Mergers: An Agency Theory Perspective on the Role of Representatives," *Academy of Management Journal*, Volume 37, Issue 3, pp. 703-721.

King, D., and Santoski, D. (Dec. 1997). "Making Mergers Work," *Canadian Insurance*, Volume 102, Issue 13, pp. 16-18.

King, J. (Aug. 1998). "Amoco Merger Marries IT Opposites," *Computerworld*, Volume 32, Issue 33, pp. 1, 76.

Kirk, J., and Miller, M.A. (1986). *Reliability and Validity in Qualitative Research*, Sage Publications, Newbury Park, California.

Klein, A., Rosenfeld, J., and Beranek, W. (Dec. 1991). "The Two Stages of an Equity Carve-outs and the Price Response of Parent and Subsidiary Stock," *Managerial & Decision Economics*, Volume 12, Issue 6, pp. 449-460.

Kosnik, R.D., and Shapiro, D.L. (Feb. 1997). "Agency Conflict Between Investment Banks and Corporate Clients in Merger and Acquisition Transactions: Causes & Remedies," *Academy of Management Executive*, Volume 11, Issue 1, pp 7-20.

KPMG Management Consulting. (1999). *Mergers & Acquisitions in Europe Research Report,* London.

Krippendorff, K. (1984). *Content Analysis: An Introduction to Its Methodology*, Sage Publications. Newbury Park, California.

Kroll, M., Wright, P., Toombs, L., and Leavell, H. (Feb. 1997). "Form of Control: A Critical Determinant of Acquisition Performance and CEO Rewards," *Strategic Management Journal*, Volume 18, Issue 2, pp. 85-96.

Krouse, C.L., Danger, K.L., Cabolis, C., and Carter, T.D. (Apr. 1999). "The Bell System Divestiture/Deregulation and the Efficiency of the Operating Companies," *Journal of Law and Economics*, Volume 42, Issue 1, pp. 61-87.

Lane, P.J., Cannella, A.A. Jr., and Lubatkin, M.H. (June 1998). "Agency Problems as Antecedents to Unrelated Mergers and Diversification: Amihud and Lev Reconsidered," *Strategic Management Journal*, Volume 19, Issue 6, pp. 555-578.

Larsson, R., and Finkelstein, S. (Jan./Feb. 1999). "Integrating Strategic, Organisational and Human Resource Perspectives on Mergers and Acquisitions: A Case Survey of Synergy Realisation," *Organisation Science*, Volume 10, Issue 1, pp. 1-25.

Lasfer, M.A., Sudarsanam, S., and Taffler, R.J. (Autumn 1996). "Financial Distress, Asset Sales, and Lender Monitoring," *Financial Management*, Volume 25, Issue 3, pp. 57-66.

Leslie, K.J., and Michaels, M. (Jan. 1998). "The Real Power of Real Options," *Corporate Finance*, Issue 158, pp. 13-20.

Lewis-Beck, M.S. (1995). *Data Analysis: An Introduction.* Sage Publications, Thousand Oaks, California.

Light, D.A. (Mar./Apr. 1999). "Acquisitions: Can You Learn from Experience?," *Harvard Business Review*, Volume 77, Issue 2, pp. 18-19.

Lins, K., and Servaes, H. (Dec. 1999). "International Evidence on the Value of Corporate Diversification," *The Journal of Finance*, Volume 54, Issue 6, pp. 2215-2239.

Locke, K. (2001). *Grounded Theory in Management Research*, Sage Publications, London, England.

Loderer, C., and Martin, K. (Winter 1990). "Corporate Acquisitions by Listed Firms: The Experience of a Comprehensive Sample," *Financial Management*, Volume 19, Issue 4, pp. 17-33.

Loughran, T., and Vijh, A.M. (Dec. 1997). "Do Long-term Shareholders Benefit from Corporate Acquisitions," *Journal of Finance*, Volume 52, Issue 5, pp. 1765-1790.

Lynk, W.J. (Oct. 1995). "Non-profit Hospital Mergers and the Exercise of the Market Power," *Journal of Law and Economics*, Volume 38, Issue 2, pp. 437-462.

Lys, T., and Vincent, L. (Oct./Nov. 1995). "An Analysis of Value Destruction in AT&T's Acquisition of NCR," *Journal of Financial Economics*, Volume 39, Issue 2/3, pp. 353-378.

McClenahen, John S. (Jan. 18, 1999). "How Much Value Creation?," *Industry Week*, Cleveland, Volume 248, Issue 2, p. 9.

McClelland, S. (Sept 1998). "The Twilight Zone," *Telecommunications*, Volume 32, Issue 9, p. 6.

McKiernan, P., and Merali, Y. (Aug. 1995). "Integrating Information Systems After a Merger," *Long Range Planning*, Volume 28, Issue 4, pp. 54-62.

McLaughlin, R.M. (Oct. 1992). "Does the Form of Compensation Matter? Investment Banker Fee Contracts in Tender Offers," *Journal of Financial Economics*, Volume 32, Issue 2, pp. 223-260.

Macquieira, C.P., Megginson, W.L., and Nail, L. (1998). "Wealth Creation versus Wealth Redistribution in Pure Stock for Stock Mergers," *Journal of Financial Economics*, Volume 48, Issue 1, pp. 3-33.

Maksimovic, V., and Philips, G. (Dec. 2001). "The Market for Corporate Assets: Who Engages in Mergers and Asset Sales and are There Efficiency Gains?," *Journal of Finance*, Volume 56, Issue 6, pp. 2019-2066.

Malatesta, P.H. (April 1983). "The Wealth Effects of Merger Activity and the Objective Function of Merging Firms," *Journal of Financial Economics*, Volume 11, Issue 1-4, pp. 155-181.

Manson, S., Stark, A.W., and Thomas, H.M. (April 1993). A Cash Flow Analysis of the Operational Gains from Takeovers, University of Essex. Working Paper.

Martin, K.J. (Sept. 1996). "The Method of Payment in Corporate Acquisitions, Investment Opportunities and Management Ownership," *Journal of Finance*, Volume 51, Issue 4, pp. 1227-1246.

May, D.O. (Sept. 1995). "Do Managerial Motives Influence Firm Risk Reduction Strategies?," *Journal of Finance*, Volume 50, Issue 4, pp. 1291-1307.

Michel, A., Shaked, I., and Lee, You-Tay. (Summer 1991). "An Evaluation of Investment Banker Acquisition Advice: The Shareholders' Perspective," *Financial Management,* Volume 20, Issue 2, pp. 40-50.

Mikkelson, W.H., and Partch, M. (1997). "The Decline of Takeovers and Disciplinary Managerial Turnover," *Journal of Financial Economics*, Volume 44, Issue 2, pp. 205-228.

Millwand, L., and Brewerton, P. (2001). *Organisational Research Methods*, Sage Publications, London, England.

Mitchell, Mark L., and Mulherin, J.H. (1996). "The Impact of Industry Shocks on Takeover and Restructuring Activity," *Journal of Financial Economics*, Volume 41, Issue 2, pp. 193-229.

Montgomery, C.A. (1994). "Corporate Diversification," *Journal of Economic Perspectives*, Volume 8, Issue 3, 163-78.

Morck, R., Shleifer, A., and Vishny, R.W. (Mar 1990). "Do Managerial Objectives Drive Bad Acquisitions?," *Journal of Finance*, Volume 45, Issue 1, pp. 31-48.

Morgan, G., and Smircich, L. (1980). "The Case for Qualitative Research," *Academy of Management Review*, Volume 5, Issue 4, pp. 491-500.

Naccarato, J.L., and Neundorf, K.A. (1998). "Content Analysis as a Predictive Methodology: Recall, Readership and Evaluations of Business-to-Business Print Advertising," *Journal of Advertising Research*, Volume 38, Issue 3, pp. 19-33.

Naman, J.L., and Slevin, D.P. (1993). "Entrepreneurship and the Concept of Fit: A Model and Empirical Tests," *Strategic Management Journal*, Volume 14, Issue 2, pp. 137-154.

Nathan, K., and Dunne, K. (1991). "The Purchase Pooling Choice: Some Explanatory Variables," *Journal of Accounting and Public Policy*, Volume 10, Issue 4, page 309.

Nayyar, P.R. (1992). "On the Measurement of Corporate Diversification Strategy: Evidence form Large U.S. Service Firms," *Strategic Management Journal*, Volume 13, Issue 3, pp. 219-236.

Neter, J., Wasserman, W., and Whitmore, G.A. (1973). *Fundamental Statistics for Business and Economics*. Fourth Edition. Allyon and Bacon, Boston, Massachusetts.

Newman, I., and Benz, C.R. (1998). *Qualitative-Quantitative Research Methodology: Exploring the Interactive Continuum.* Southern Illinois Press, Carbondale, Illinois.

Norburn, D., and Schoenberg, R. (1994). "European Cross-border Acquisition: How Was it for You?" *Long Range Planning*, Volume27, Issue 4, pp. 25-34.

Nygaard, L.B. (April 2002). "Mergers and Acquisitions Beyond Due Diligence," *Internal Auditor*, pp. 37-43.

O'Sullivan, L., and Geringer, J.M. (Apr 1993). "Harnessing the Power of Your Value Chain," *Long Range Planning,* Volume 26, Issue 2, pp. 59-68.

Overman, S. (Aug 1999). "Learning Your M & ABC's," *HR Focus*, Volume 76, Issue 8, pp. 7-8.

Paul, C.E. Jr. (Mar/Apr 1995). "Scouting the M&A Landscape for Quality Targets," *Mergers and Acquisitions*, Volume 29, Issue 5, p. 20.

Philippatos, G.C., and Baird III, P.L. (1996). "Post-merger Performance, Managerial Superiority and the Market for Corporate Control," *Managerial and Decision Economics*, Volume 17, Issue 1, pp. 45-55.

Porter, M. (1985). *Competitive Advantage*, Free Press, New York.

Potter, W.J., and Levine-Donnerstein, D. (Aug 1999). "Rethinking Validity and Reliability in Content Analysis," *Journal of Applied Communication Research*, Volume 27, Issue 3, pp. 258-284.

Powell, R.G. (1997). "Modelling Takeover Likelihood," *Journal of Business Finance & Accounting*, Volume 24, Issue 7&8, pp. 1009-1030.

Rajan, R., Servaes, H., and Zingales, L. (Feb. 2000). "The Cost of Diversity: The Diversification Discount and Inefficient Investment," *The Journal of Finance*, Volume 55, Issue 1, pp. 35-80.

Rao, P.R., and Vermaelen, T. (1998). "Glamour, Value and the Post-acquisition Performance of Acquiring Firms," *Journal of Financial Economics*, Volume 49, Issue 2, pp. 223-253.

Rau, P. R. (2000). "Investment Bank Market Share, Contingent Fee Payments and the Performance of the Acquiring Firms," *The Journal of Financial Economics*, Volume 56, pp. 293-324.

Ravenscraft, D.J., and Scherer, F.M. (1991). "Divisional Sell-off: A Hazard Function Analysis," *Managerial & Decision Economics*, Volume 12, Issue 6, pp. 429-438.

Raymond, P. (1997). *Business Policy*, The Institute of Internal Auditors – UK, London.

Reidel, R. (2000). *Research Strategies for Secondary Data: A Perspective for Criminology and Criminal Justice*, Sage Publications, Thousand Oaks, California.

Reilly, A.H., Brett, J.M., and Stroh, L.K. (1993). "The Impact of Corporate Turbulence on Managers' Attitudes," *Strategic Management Journal* , Volume 14, Special Issue, pp. 167-179.

Reimann, B.C. (1989). "Creating Value to Keep the Raiders at Bay," *Long Range Planning*, Volume 22, Issue 3, pp. 18-27.

Renecker, M.A. (1993). "A Qualitative Study of Information Seeking Among Members of an Academic Community: Methodological Issues and Problems," *Library Quarterly*, Volume 63, Issue 4, pp. 487-507.

Roberts, C.W. (2000). "A Conceptual Framework for Quantitative Text Analysis," *Quality & Quantity*, Volume 34 (3), pp. 259-274.

Robins, J., and Wiersema, M.F. (May 1995). "A Resource-based Approach to the Multi-business Firm: Empirical Analysis of Portfolio Interrelationships and Corporate Financial Performance," *Strategic Management Journal*, Volume 16, Issue 4, pp. 277-299.

Robins, S.S., and Stylianou, A.C. (1999). "Post-merger Systems Integration: The Impact of IS Capabilities," *Information & Management*, Volume 36, Issue 4, pp. 205-212.

Robinson, J.R., and Shane, P.B. (1990). "Acquisition Accounting Method and Bid Premium for Target Firms," *Accounting Review*, Volume 65, Issue 1, pp. 25-48.

Roll, R. (1988). "Empirical Evidence on Takeover Activity and Shareholder Wealth in Coffee," J.C., Lowenstein, L. & Ackerman, S.R., (Ed.) *Knights, Raiders & Targets*, Oxford University Press Inc., Boston, Massachusetts.

Rose, P.S. (1995). "The Distribution of Outcomes from Corporate Mergers: Evidence from Commercial Bank Acquisition Strategies," *Journal of Accounting, Auditing & Finance*, Volume 10, Issue 2, pp. 343-361.

Rouse, M.J., and Daellenbach, U.S. (1999). "Rethinking Research Methods for the Resource-based Perspective: Isolating Sources of Sustainable Competitive Advantage," *Strategic Management Journal*, Volume 20, Issue 5, pp. 487-194.

Sadtler, D.R. (1993). "Brief Case: The Long Road to Parenting Advantage," *Long Range Planning*, Volume 26, Issue 2, pp. 125-127.

Salami, A.R., and Sudarsanam, S. (1999). Financing Corporate Acquisitions: Relevance of the Accounting Policy Choice, City University. Working paper.

Saunders, M., Lewis, P., and Thornhill, A. (1997). *Research Methods for Business Students*, Pitman, London, England.

Sawyer, S. (2001). Analysis by Long Walk: Some Approaches to the Synthesis of Multiple Sources of Evidence. In Trends in the Choice of Qualitative Methods. Ed. Trauth, E.M., pp. 163-190, Idea Group Publishing, Hershey, Pennsylvania.

Schipper, K., and Thompson, R. (April 1983). "Evidence on the Capitalised Value of Merger Activity for Acquiring Firms," *Journal of Financial Economics*, Volume 11, Issue 1-4, pp. 85-119.

Schnieder, S.C., and Dunbar, R.L.M. (1992). "A Psychological Reading of Hostile Takeover Attempts," *Academy of Management Review*, Volume 17, Issue 3, pp. 527-568.

Schoenberg, R., and Reeves, R. (1999). "What Determines Acquisition Activity within an Industry?," *European Management Journal*, Volume 17, Issue 1, pp. 93-98.

Schwab, D.P. (1999). *Research Methods for Organizational Investigation*, Lawrence Erlbaum Associates, Mahwah, New Jersey.

Schwert, G.W. (1996). "Markup Pricing in Mergers and Acquisitions," *Journal of Financial Economics*, Volume 41, Issue 2, pp. 153-192.

Seale, C. (1999). *The Quality of Qualitative Research.* Sage Publications, London, England.

Servaes, H. (Sept. 1996). "The Value of Diversification During the Conglomerate Merger Wave," *Journal of Finance*, Volume 51, Issue 4, pp. 1201-1225.

Servaes, H., and Zenner, M. (Autumn 1996). "The Role of Investment Banks in Acquisitions," *Review of Financial Studies*, Volume 9, Issue 3, pp. 787-815.

Seth, A. (Feb. 1990). "Value Creation in Acquisitions: A Re-examination of Performance Issues," *Strategic Management Journal*, Volume 11, Issue 2, pp. 99-115.

Shanley, M.T. (1992). "Agreement Between Top Management Teams and Expectations for Post Acquisition Performance," *Strategic Management Journal*, Volume 13, Issue 4, pp. 245-266.

Shaw, I.F. (1999). *Qualitative Evaluation*. Sage Publications, London, England.

Shivdasani, A. (1993). "Board Composition, Ownership Structure and Hostile Takeovers," *Journal of Accounting and Economics*, Volume 16, Issue 1-3, pp. 167-198.

Shleifer, A., and Vishny, R.W. (Winter 1991). "Takeovers in the '60s and the '80s: Evidence and Implications," *Strategic Management Journal*, Volume 12, pp. 51-59.

Sikora, M. (2000). "Gearing M & A to Meet 21st Century Demands," *Mergers and Acquisitions*, Volume 35, Issue 8, pp. 6-12.

Silverman, D. (2001). *Interpreting Qualitative Data*. Second Edition, Sage Publications, London, England.

Singh, K. (1995). "The Impact of Technological Complexity and Interfirm Cupertino on Business Survival," *Academy of Management Journal*, Volume 40, Issue 2, pp. 339-368.

Singh, H. (1993). "Challenges in Researching Corporate Restructuring," *Journal of Management Studies*, Volume 30, Issue 1, pp. 147-173.

Sirower, M.L. (1998). "Constructing a Synergistic Base for Premier Deals," *Mergers and Acquisitions*, Volume 32, Issue 6, pp. 42-49.

Smith, K.W., and Triantis, A.J. (1994). "Untapped Options for Creating Value in Acquisitions," *Mergers & Acquisitions*, Volume 29, Issue 3, pp. 17-22.

Song, M.H., and Walkling, R.A. (1993). "The Impact of Managerial Ownership on Acquisition Attempts and Target Shareholder Wealth," *JFQA*, Volume 28, Issue 4, pp. 439-458.

Sudarsanam, S., and Salami, A. (1999). Does it Matter Who Your Banker Is? Impact of Investment Bank Reputation in Takeovers, Cranfield University. Working Paper.

Sudarsanam, P.S. (1995). "The Role of Defensive Strategies and Ownership Structure of Target Firms: Evidence from UK Hostile Takeover Bids," *European Financial Management*, Volume 1, Issue 3, pp. 223-240.

Sudarsanam, S., Holl, P., and Salami, A. (1996). "Shareholder Wealth Gains in Mergers: Effect of Synergy and Ownership Structure," *Journal of Business Finance & Accounting*, Volume 23, Issue 5,6, pp. 673-698.

Thomas, H., and Pollock, T. (Jun 1999). "From I-O Economics' S-C-P Paradigm through Strategic Groups to Competence-based Competition: Reflections on the Puzzle of Competitive Strategy," *British Journal of Management*, Volume 10, Issue 2, pp. 127-140.

Trampe, J. (1998). "Thriving on Change: The Internal Auditor's role in Mergers & Acquisitions," *Journal of Accounting*, Volume 185, Issue 4, pp. 33-37.

Urquhart, C. (2001). An Encounter with Grounded Theory: Tackling the Practical and Philosophical Issues. In Trends in the Choice of Qualitative Methods. Ed. Trauth, E.M., pp.104-140, *Idea Group Publishing,* Hershey, Pennsylvania.

Varaiya, N.P. (1987). "Determinants of Premiums in Acquisition Transactions," *Managerial & Decision Economics*, Volume 8, Issue 3, pp. 175-184.

Very, P., Lubatkin, M., Calori, R., and Veiga, J. (1997). "Relative Standing and the Performance of Recently Acquired European Firms," *Strategic Management Journal*, Volume 18, Issue 8, pp. 593-614.

Very, P. (1993). "Success in Diversification: Building on Core Competences," *Long Range Planning*, Volume 26, Issue 5, pp. 80-92.

Weber, R.P. (Spring/Summer 1984). "Computer-aided Content Analysis: A Short Primer," *Qualitative Sociology*, Volume 7, Issue 1-2, pp. 126-147.

Weber, Y., and Pliskin, N. (May 1996). "The Effects of Information Systems Integration and Organisational Culture on a Firm's Effectiveness," *Information & Management*, Volume 30, Issue 30, pp. 81-90.

Weisbach, M.S. (1995). "CEO Turnover and the Firm's Investment Decisions," *Journal of Financial Economics*, Volume 37, Issue 2, pp. 159-188.

Weston, J.F., and Jawien, P.S. (1999). "Perspectives on Mergers and Restructuring," *Business Economics*, Volume 34, Issue 1, pp. 29-33.

Wiersema, L. (1995). "Perspectives on Mergers and Restructuring," *Strategic Management Journal*, Volume 16, Issue 6, pp. 447-460.

Winter, S.G. (1995). *Four R's of Profitability: Rents, Resources, Routines and Replication, In Resource-based and Evolutionary Theories of the Firm*. Kluwer Academic Publishers, Montgomery, California.

Wolcott, H.F. (1990). *Writing Up Qualitative Research*. Sage Publications, Newbury Park, California.

Woodward, S. (1997). *Managing Organisational Change*, The Institute of Internal Auditors – UK, London, England.

Yin, R.K. (1993). *Applications of Case Study Research*. Sage Publications, Thousand Oaks, California.

Young, D., and Sutcliffe, B. (Aug. 1990). "Value Gaps – Who is Right? – The Raiders, the Market or the Managers," *Long Range Planning*, Volume 23, Issue 4, pp. 30-34.

Zolkos, R. (1994). "Risk Managers Can Play a Big Role in Mergers," *Business Insurance*, Volume 28, Issue 18, pp. 24-25.

IIA Research Foundation Board of Trustees

IIA Research Foundation Board of Research Advisors

IIA RESEARCH FOUNDATION

Chairman's Circle

AT&T Corporation
Cargill, Inc.
Entergy Services, Inc.
ExxonMobil Corporation
JCPenney Company, Inc.
Microsoft Corporation
PricewaterhouseCoopers LLP
Southern Company Services, Inc.